The Romance of the Western Chamber

REISSUED FOR THE

COLUMBIA COLLEGE PROGRAM

OF TRANSLATIONS FROM

THE ORIENTAL CLASSICS

Wm. Theodore de Bary, Editor

西廂記

熊式一譯

舊雀鸎真

宋畫院待詔陳居中寫

PORTRAIT OF TS'UI YING-YING

The Romance of the Western Chamber

Translated by S. I. Hsiung

Columbia University Press

New York and London 1968

UNESCO Collection of Representative Works
Chinese Series
This book
has been accepted
in the Chinese Series
of the Translation Collection
of the United Nations
Educational, Scientific and Cultural Organization
(UNESCO)

Library of Congress Catalog Card Number: 68-22412
Printed in the United States of America

To

SIR JAMES H. STEWART LOCKHART
K.C.M.G., LL.D.

In Gratitude for his Help and Encouragement

FOREWORD

The Romance of the Western Chamber is one of the Translations from the Oriental Classics by which the Committee on Oriental Studies has sought to transmit to Western readers representative works of the major Asian traditions in thought and literature. These are works which in our judgment any educated man should have read. Frequently, however, this reading has been denied him by the lack of suitable translations. All too often he has had to choose between excerpts in popular anthologies on the one hand, and on the other heavily annotated translations intended primarily for the specialist, which in many cases are out of date or out of print. Here we offer translations of whole works written for the general reader as well as the specialist.

S. I. Hsiung's translation of *The Romance of the Western Chamber* (*Hsi-hsiang chi*) is one of a very few which have suitably presented the classic works of Chinese drama in English. Since it went out of print, this standard work has disappeared from the reading lists of courses dealing with the major works of Chinese literature. Its reprinting in this series, with a new introduction by Professor C. T. Hsia, meets a need felt for some years by the Columbia College Program in the Oriental Humanities and also follows a recommendation of the Committee for the Study of Chinese Civilization of the American Council of Learned Societies. In this latter connection the initiative taken by Professor Cyril Birch of the University of California, Berkeley, was particularly instrumental.

WM. THEODORE DE BARY

A CRITICAL INTRODUCTION

THROUGH the centuries a number of love stories have delighted the Chinese both as literature and as popular entertainment. Among these the story of Scholar Chang and Ts'ui Ying-ying holds a unique place of honor not only because of its continuing popularity as a repertoire piece in the regionally diversified Chinese theater but because, in the course of its evolution from roughly 800 to 1300, it has been thrice embodied in an imperishable masterpiece: Yuan Chen's tale in the classical style, "The Story of Ying-ying" (*Ying-ying chuan*); [1] Tung Chich-yuan's (Scholar Tung's) long narrative poem, *The Romance of the Western Chamber* (*Hsi-hsiang chi*), and Wang Shih-fu's play of the same title. No other Chinese love story has enjoyed comparable literary distinction. It is true that Emperor Hsüan-tsung's infatuation for Yang Kuei-fei has been celebrated in at least an equal number of classics: Po Chü-i's *Ch'ang-hen ko* (The song of everlasting regret), the Yuan playwright Po P'u's *Wu-t'ung yü* (Rain on the wu-t'ung tree), and the Ch'ing playwright Hung Sheng's *Ch'ang-sheng tien* (The palace of long life). But the two plays cannot claim the pivotal literary importance of Wang Shih-fu's *Hsi-hsiang chi,* while Po Chü-i's poem is a mere ballad in comparison with Tung Chieh-yuan's love epic.

Yang Kuei-fei, an imperial favorite killed upon the outbreak of a major revolt, was a legend even during

[1] Readers unfamiliar with the tale are advised to read Mr. Hsiung's translation on pp. 271–81 before proceeding with this introduction.

her lifetime: her tragic story naturally attracted poets, storytellers, and playwrights. Ying-ying, however, would have remained an unsung beauty if Yuan Chen had not recorded her story. Though in the tale both her unusual refinement and her distinguished family name suggest an aristocratic upbringing (in Tung's poem she is identified as a prime minister's daughter), scholars now agree that the tale is disguised autobiography and that Ying-ying was in real life a girl of humbler social status with whom the author was once in love. After Yuan Chen went to Ch'ang-an (as does Scholar Chang in the tale), he found it to his advantage to discontinue the affair. Despite their romantic propensities, young poets and scholars residing in the capital in Yuan Chen's time were determined to succeed, and they were equally ambitious to earn top honors at the examinations and to form matrimonial ties that would prove highly advantageous to their future career. Yuan Chen was extraordinarily successful: a poet enjoying equal fame with his close friend Po Chü-i, he soon earned the *chin-shih* degree, married a daughter of the prominent Wei family, and eventually reached the position of prime minister.

In recording the story of Ying-ying, Yuan Chen must have been driven by remorse or a sense of regret. At the same time, however, the writing of such tales (*ch'uan-ch'i*) was a social act designed to win the admiration of one's literary friends and earn the approval of the senior members of the national elite. Even if he had wanted to, Yuan could not have written a confession containing all the details of his courtship and desertion. He therefore invented a scholar Chang (Chang Sheng) as the hero and, according to the rules of the genre, included many poems and a few set

pieces of rhetoric in the tale. Even Ying-ying's touching letter was probably his own composition designed
to show his mastery of the epistolary style. Modern
readers have always been bothered by the hero's lame
and unfeeling apology for his desertion. But Yuan must
have branded the sensitive and unassuming heroine a
dangerous vixen worthy to be classed with the notori-
ous kingdom-wreckers of the past to impress his readers with his brilliance at argumentation.

Despite its unconvincing attempt to defend the hero,
however, the tale has retained a core of truth, and it
moves us (as it must have moved its contemporary
readers) for its portrayal of an enigmatic and fascina-
ting girl of compelling credibility. Ying-ying is not the
typical forsaken woman in Chinese poetry—a courtesan, a merchant's wife, or a palace lady waiting helplessly in her boudoir for the absent lover. Nor is she
the conventional heroine of romantic pluck and matrimonial good fortune. By Yuan Chen's time several
romantic scholar-lovers have become folklore figures,
the most famous being the Han writer Ssu-ma Hsiang-
ju, whose lute playing persuaded the young widow
Cho Wen-chün to elope with him, against the wishes
of her rich father. In both the Tung and the Wang
versions of *Hsi-hsiang chi,* Scholar Chang repeatedly
identifies himself with Ssu-ma Hsiang-ju and other
romantic seducers and compares his beloved to Cho
Wen-chün, but in the tale Ying-ying is not a young
widow knowledgeable about love and resolute in her
pursuit of happiness. Eager to respond to her suitor,
she nevertheless gives him a stern lecture upon their
first assignation, although soon afterwards she yields
to his ardor voluntarily, forgetting both her maidenly
reserve and her traditional regard for propriety. In

her apparent contradiction Yuan Chen has caught for all time the dilemma of every properly brought up Chinese girl faced with the supreme temptation.

In both versions of *Hsi-hsiang chi* the characterization of Ying-ying is much fuller. She shows a strain of slyness, rationalizes her rudeness toward Scholar Chang on their first tryst, and gives vent to her strong indignation against her double-dealing mother. She also conveys her varied moods of expectancy, languor, and dejection in some of the loveliest stanzas of verse. But with all this new wealth of lyrical and dramatic detail, neither Tung nor Wang succeeds in giving us a more complex portrait of the heroine mainly because, as the daughter of a late prime minister, she is further removed from the milieu of her prototype, and her apprehension and insecurity both during Scholar Chang's courtship and after his departure to Ch'ang-an appear to be less firmly rooted in social reality. Despite her ambiguous family background, Yuan Chen's Ying-ying retains the essential vulnerability of a gentle girl turned mistress because of her overgenerosity to her lover. She makes no further move to influence him after he has failed to reply to her letter, and a year later she marries. But her refusal to see Chang after they both have married ends the story on a haunting note of unsentimental realism. Little wonder that, as a new type of heroine in Chinese literature, she was showered with sympathy and admiration in numerous poems and song cycles by T'ang and Sung poets.

During the Northern Sung, which saw the rise of many types of popular entertainment, storytellers took over the tale of Ying-ying and gave it a new lease of life. We must agree with some recent scholars, however, in assuming that, with their understandable sympathy for the heroine, their rather unsophisticated audiences could not have stomached the tale as Yuan Chen wrote it and would have wanted either a more tragic ending or a happier one, with the caddish hero duly transformed into a devoted lover. The storytellers apparently took the latter option, and during the years (1190–1208) when Emperor Chang-tsung of the Chin dynasty ruled over North China their version finally got written down in Tung Chieh-yuan's magnificent poem of eight books and over fifty thousand characters. The reformed hero, Chang Kung (courtesy name: Chün-jui), dominates the poem. He eventually marries Ying-ying after his rival Cheng Heng has been exposed as a malicious liar.

Tung's *Hsi-hsiang chi* is the only extant example of a complete work in the genre of *chu-kung-tiao*. The term, meaning "medley," refers to the main feature of the work lyrical stanzas set to tunes in various keys. In addition to describing scenery and action, these songs and song sequences delineate the psychological conditions of the characters and reproduce their soliloquies and conversations. In an actual performance, therefore, the narrator must be something of a dramatic interpreter as he in turn impersonates Scholar Chang, Ying-ying, or her maid Hung Niang and conveys their thoughts and words in song. After singing one, two, or three songs, he recites a passage which serves to summarize a situation, forward the plot or, occasionally, introduce a note of suspense. These passages are usually brief except when they include dialogue or quotations from earlier versions of the story, such as Yuan Chen's tale and his friend Li Shen's "Song of Ying-ying" (*Ying-ying ko*).

Tung's *Hsi-hsiang chi* is without doubt the greatest narrative poem in the Chinese language. Though Wang Shih-fu's play has always enjoyed far greater fame and popularity, partly because Tung's poem was for a long time not generally available, it is difficult to maintain that the play, which has adapted nearly all the episodes from the poem and numerous passages of its verse, is necessarily the greater work of the two. For one thing, the hero of Tung's poem answers to a more serious conception of the lover, even though his lovesickness exposes him time and again to situations of genuine humor. The hero of the play, while basically as much of a naïve and ardent lover, is blemished by levity and assumes in some of his scenes the guise of an ineffectual and boastful seducer.[2] If Yuan Chen has permanently fixed the image of Ying-ying, it is entirely to Tung's credit that Scholar Chang has become in his own right a beloved figure and an archetype for the romantic scholar-hero to be seen in subsequent Chinese drama and fiction. He is not at all points believable, and to Western readers used to romantic heroes of greater self-assertiveness he may appear too easily despondent, too ready to commit suicide, and toward the end too cowardly in the face of Cheng Heng's challenge. But in all his important scenes, subsequently adapted in Wang's play, he engages our affection and sympathy. Certainly no previous Chinese author has ever caught the changeable states of a young man in love, by turns enraptured and dejected, tender and silly, with as much precision in such a copious volume of impassioned verse.

In *Hsi-hsiang chi* Tung Chieh-yuan has wrought a new kind of romance—the romance of the gifted scholar (*ts'ai-tzu*) and the gifted beauty (*chia-jen*). But the label is somewhat misleading since Scholar

[2] Cf. Chang Hsin-chang, "The West Chamber: The Theme of Love in Chinese Drama," *Annual of the China Society of Singapore* (1957), pp. 9–19.

Chang and Ying-ying are seen primarily as passionate lovers. They are of course paragons of beauty and talent and they both come from distinguished families (in the poem as in the play Scholar Chang has become the impoverished son of a late minister of rites). But in a sense their heredity and family background merely certify their capacity for the intensest kind of love experience. By the same token of logic, those who are either ill-bred, gross in their features, or lacking in literary culture cannot love with poetic warmth, as is obviously the case with the rebel leader Sun Fei-hu and the hideous Cheng Heng, both of whom covet Ying-ying's person without possessing an iota of the delicacy and tenderness befitting her lover. Once a gifted scholar meets a gifted beauty, they fall in love as a matter of course. Because of the homogeneity of their culture and because they are denied the right of free courtship, they do not need nor would they have the time for the kind of dates which provide modern lovers the opportunity to explore personality and background and to ascertain if their initial attraction for each other makes for lifelong compatibility. By modern standards Scholar Chang's courtship of Ying-ying is extremely brief. During their second meeting (he has merely caught a glimpse of her at their first chance encounter) she already shows her strong interest by reciting a poem in response to his, and in Wang's adaptation of the poem (Part II, Act 1) lines descriptive of Chang's melancholy following the exchange of poems are subtly reassigned to Ying-ying to indicate that she, too, misses him. She has fallen in love and, given her predisposition to reciprocate, it suffices her to know that the handsome scholar is sincere and ardent and can convey his feelings through poetry and, later, the music of the lute.

For both scholar and beauty, however, if their literary education prepares them for love, they have been since early childhood conditioned by their Confucian upbringing to respect propriety and to prepare diligently for their future roles in society. Neither Scholar Chang nor Ying-ying is a conscious rebel, but what is most endearing about them is that, driven by their hunger for love, they are able at least temporarily to disregard counsels of prudence and to risk parental and social disapproval. Once a scholar earns his *chin-shih* degree, he is assured of worldly success, and high officials will be only too happy to marry their daughters to him. He may marry happily, but he will have missed the agony and rapture of being held captive by love. While every Chinese scholar wants to compete in the examinations to prove his worth and earn his deserved place in society, the more romantically inclined would count it as his good fortune if he could seek love on his own and be loved for his own sake before his worth is certified by a degree. Scholar Chang may appear too sentimental by Western standards, but he distinguishes himself precisely by his total submission to the dictates of love, by his shameless exhibition of all the symptoms of lovesickness (initial high spirits, loss of appetite, languor and sleeplessness, suicidal thoughts, revival of high spirits upon the least sign that his fortune has changed for the better). In a Chinese romance these symptoms alone are enough to move the young lady to pity and love.

She is ready to pity and love because, among daughters of good families, few indeed are privileged to be courted clandestinely or to have a love intrigue. While the young scholar moves about a good deal to attend the examinations and can find genuine love or at least sexual solace in the arms of a courtesan, the young lady stays home, applies herself to needlework (since there is little else she is called upon to do), and watches the seasons go by until it is time for her to assume a more useful role as wife. It requires an act of imagination on our part, therefore, to realize the wild agitation she undergoes if someone should address a poem to her, serenade her at night, or send her a billet-doux. Ying-ying, moreover, is unusually lucky because she is lodging in a temple and is therefore more liable to attract attention. Had she lived at home, she would have had no choice but to marry the youth her parents had chosen for her. While she may live a reasonably happy life with him (since her fiancé Cheng Heng is obviously a gross caricature), she would nevertheless have been denied the tumultuous experience of being wooed and loved which she has in the temple.

Upon the discovery of his clandestine affair, Scholar Chang is ordered by Ying-ying's mother to go to the capital to take the examinations. But even without such prompting he would sooner or later bestir himself, and his beloved, while reluctant to be parted from him, would not think of stopping him. Theirs is not the motto, "All for love, or the world well lost": they will want to return to the world after they have enjoyed love in its despite. Furthermore, even for the most passionate lovers, their ardor feeds upon secrecy and opposition. But in time the secret will be out, the opposition will relent in the face of a scandal, and the lovers themselves will want to rectify their relationship. The scholar has now to earn his academic honors to make up for his earlier course of romantic nonconformity and to vindicate the beauty's honor. Since he usually has no difficulty in doing so, the erstwhile romantic lovers will settle into a happy marriage and rear talented children who, it may be hoped, will in time have romances of their own.

All scholar-beauty romances end happily, though until the last possible moment their authors want to keep us worried over the possibility of the lovers' not being able to achieve a lasting union. As a pioneer of the genre, however, Tung Chieh-yuan is not yet up to the game of suspense. He prevents Scholar Chang from marrying Ying-ying by postponing his return from Ch'ang-an and by creating a new villain, Cheng Heng, who has a legal claim to her hand. After Scholar Chang has achieved high honors as the third-highest-ranking *chin-shih* at the examinations, he falls unaccountably ill and Ying-ying anxiously awaits news of him. (In reading Chinese romances of this type, one has the feeling that much of the suffering would have been spared if the lovers could have made long-distance telephone calls or at least entrusted their messages to a more efficient postal service.) She sends him the famous letter, duly copied from Yuan Chen's tale, itemizing the sentimental meaning of all her accompanying presents. But since the loving hero, unlike his prototype in the tale, does not deserve her reproach and mistrust, the pathos occasioned by the sending and reading of the letter appears contrived. Then Cheng Heng arrives on the scene, convinces Ying-ying's mother that Chang has married some girl in Ch'ang-an, and almost succeeds in marrying Ying-ying. Chang, who arrives too late to clear his good name, escapes with Ying-ying to the headquarters of General Tu, who intervenes in his friend's behalf as he had done once earlier during the rioting soldiers' siege of the temple. Out of shame, Cheng Heng hurls himself down a flight of stone steps and dies. (In the play he dies even more conveniently by knocking his head against a tree.) A brief review of the later episodes would indicate that Tung has unnecessarily complicated his tale to meet the requirements of a romance. The play suffers from the same fault to an even more serious extent.

Wang Shih-fu's *Hsi-hsiang chi,* composed some hundred years after Tung's poem, is a series of five Northern-style plays (*tsa-chü*). In the early Ming period Yang Ching-hsien wrote *Hsi-yu chi,* a cycle of six plays about Tripitaka's journey to the west. Aside from these two works, however, nearly all *tsa-chü* dating from the Yuan and Ming are self-contained units of four acts, with or without an additional brief scene known as *hsieh-tzu* (the wedge). In a performance the actor undertaking the principal male or female role sings throughout the four acts, though some plays require him to impersonate two parts. Other characters may sing in the wedge, usually according to prescribed tunes. All the arias in an act are in one key, and they all observe the same rhyme, a feat almost impossible to duplicate in an English translation. The playwright makes much use of dialogue and monologue; quite often even a minor character gives a lengthy account of himself when first appearing on the stage. In *Hsi-hsiang chi* most such monologues are quite short, and the 1656 edition of Chin Sheng-t'an (or Chin Shên-t'an in Mr. Hsiung's transliteration), upon which the translation is mainly based, has further abridged General Tu's long recitation in Part II, Act I (p. 66).

Wang Shih-fu would have certainly adapted Yuan Chen's tale as a four-act play if Tung Chieh-yuan had not already greatly expanded it. Instead of condensing the poem, therefore, Wang took the bold step of developing most of its episodes even more fully. The resultant work, unprecedented in its length and unsurpassed for its wealth of lyrical poetry, towers above all other Yuan plays and is rightly considered the supreme masterpiece of Chinese drama. But it is a masterpiece *manqué* if the fifth play is to be regarded as an integral part of the whole. To justify Wang Shih-fu's fair name as a playwright, tradition had early maintained that he was the author of only the first four plays and that the fifth was a continuation by Kuan (Kwang) Han-ch'ing. But Wang, who flourished during the reign of Emperor Ch'eng-tsung (1295–1307), belonged to a younger generation of playwrights than the pioneers Kuan Han-ch'ing and Po P'u. It is highly unlikely that an older man of greater fame would have wanted to complete the work of a younger contemporary. Besides, it amounts to slander to ascribe to Kuan, a great playwright of extreme versatility, something deemed unworthy of Wang.

Scholars today are content to ascribe all five plays to Wang and to blame the inferiority of the fifth upon the intractable material he inherited from Tung. Still, there is no reason why a great playwright, as Wang has proved himself to be in the first four plays, could not have adapted or altered the material more successfully. If one examines the fifth play carefully, one finds at least its fourth act disturbingly different from all preceding acts on one important point of theatrical convention. Allowing for permissible departures, in the first four plays Wang has observed the rule that only one character sings throughout an act (unfortunately, this rule is no longer apparent in the present translation because the Chin Sheng-t'an edition has incorporated every wedge with its succeeding or preceding act). He seems to have deliberately violated the rule for greater dramatic effect only in Part IV, Act 4, where Scholar Chang and Ying-ying both sing, although the latter appears only as a presence in his dream and therefore an extension of his consciousness. In Part V, Act 4, however, Chang, Ying-ying, and Hung Niang all sing (in the present translation General Tu also sings and the concluding stanzas are marked for group singing). Writing in the prime of the *tsa-chü* tradition, it would seem that Wang Shih-fu would not have violated convention without apparent justification. If the traditional assumption that Wang did not write the fifth play is not entirely groundless, then it would seem reasonable to assume that some later hand, writing in the decadence of the *tsa-chü* tradition, wrote a sequel to meet popular demand for a complete cycle of plays based on Tung's poem.

The five parts of *Hsi-hsiang chi* comprise 20 or 21 acts (the long wedge preceding Part II, Act 2 [pp. 58–72 of the present translation] is in some Ming editions given the status of an independent act). In keeping with convention, Scholar Chang enjoys the singing role in Part I as does Hung Niang in Part III. In Part II Hung Niang sings in Act 2 while Ying-ying sings in the remaining acts. Scholar Chang is assigned the singing role in Acts 1 and 4 of Part IV, while Hung Niang and Ying-ying sing respectively in Acts 2 and 3. In Part V the singing roles for Acts 1–3 belong respectively to Ying-ying, Chang, and Hung Niang, while in Act 4, as has already been observed, all three sing. In enumerating the singing roles of the five plays, I may seem to have dwelt upon the obvious, but actually one cannot begin to appreciate Yuan drama unless one keeps in mind that a character is assigned the singing role usually to the exclusion of some other character who could as well have had the honor and that, once chosen, he dominates the act or play and lends it its distinctive emotional tone and dramatic unity. In Po

P'u's *Rain on the Wu-t'ung Tree,* for instance, the love relationship between Yang Kuei-fei and Hsüan-tsung is seen through the perspective of his infatuation, dotage, impotence, and desolation because the emperor is assigned the singing role. The playwright, however, could with equal justification have given that role to Yang Kuei-fei and his play would then be totally different because he would have written all the arias to accommodate the feminine point of view. In the case of *Hsi-hsiang chi,* while Scholar Chang would seem the obvious choice for the singing role in Part I because he is the dominant figure in the corresponding portion of Tung's poem, for many subsequent acts the choice of a dominant part is by no means automatic. An act assigned to Hung Niang could be with equal propriety given to Chang or Ying-ying. It speaks for the dramatic genius of Wang Shih-fu that he should have assigned the entire third play and three additional acts to Hung Niang, who would logically appear to be a character of lesser importance than either of the lovers. If Yuan Chen has been the main creator of Ying-ying and if Tung Chieh-yuan has delineated Scholar Chang's passion with a warmth and precision not surpassed in the play, then it is Wang Shih-fu's primary distinction as the final shaper of the story that he should have chosen to give Hung Niang a role actually larger than Ying-ying's and to compose for her some of the best scenes in the play. Hung Niang has already been quite important in Tung's poem, but it is only in the play that she becomes fully alive. The long-lasting influence of Wang's consummate portrayal can be seen in the fact that in nearly all versions of the play performed by regional operatic troupes all over China until the recent Proletarian Cultural Revolution Hung Niang has been awarded the principal role. In Peking opera *Hsi-hsiang chi* has been long since retitled *Hung Niang* to emphasize her central importance.

In traditional Chinese society (at least as it is reflected in fiction and drama) a young lady's closest friend is usually her personal maid to whom she can confide her secrets and entrust her important messages. Her suitor, since he cannot communicate with her directly at least until he has gained her favor, must also rely on her maid for essential services. (In some romances the suitor's page plays a similarly important role; in both versions of *Hsi-hsiang chi*, however, Scholar Chang's page plays only a minor role in the later part of the story.) No romance of the Western Chamber could have prospered without Hung Niang. "An inveterate matchmaker, Hung Niang is the liveliest as well as the most unforgettable character in the play," a recent scholar observes.[3] "She is as adept in repartee and raillery as in the stratagems of love. She knows how to tell innocent lies, how to prevaricate, to tease, to persuade, to convince, to console, and to defy." Hung Niang is certainly always on the go, and the lovers, when immobilized by lovesickness or despair, are goaded into action only because of her. But, speaking in terms of her essential dramatic function as distinct from her vital role in the plot, because she herself is not in love, Hung Niang appears perhaps even more importantly as an observer than as a doer. Ying-ying, too, observes, as in the powerful dinner scene (Part II, Act 3) where she pours forth in a long monologue her scorn for her perfidious mother and her pity for her dejected lover. But in most of her other scenes she primarily calls attention to her own melancholy and

[3] Liu Wu-chi, *An Introduction to Chinese Literature* (Bloomington and London, Indiana University Press, 1966), p. 173.

desolation as befits a heroine anchored in the sentimental tradition of *tz'u* and *ch'ü* poetry. Hung Niang, however, far more often diversifies the lyrical mood by providing an angle of observation from which to comment on the other characters in an amused, sympathetic, or indignant fashion. It is she who exposes the comic absurdity of Scholar Chang as an ineffectual and conceited lover, the unsuspected slyness of Ying-ying, the hypocrisy and stupidity of her mother, and the ridiculous pretensions of Cheng Heng. In doing so, she adds immensely to the *drama* of the play. When, for instance, we read in Tung's poem that Scholar Chang takes great pains to prepare his toilet in readiness for the dinner in his honor, we are merely amused. Wang Shih-fu has borrowed this detail from Tung in Part II, Act 2, but, by assigning the singing role to Hung Niang in that act, he defines Chang's eagerness with comic finality. When she comes to his room to invite him to dinner, Chang asks:

I have not carried a mirror with me on my travels. Could you kindly look me over and see if I am presentable?

Hung Niang comments:

I see that he is only too ready to obey the summons to the feast,[4]
But that, as he struts to and fro, he looks admiringly at his own shadow.
The crazy Graduate, the poor mad Scholar,
Has taken such pains to polish his head,
That flies might slither on it,
And its brilliance might dazzle one's eyes.
He looks such a poor, miserable wretch that he sets one's teeth on edge.

[4] This line actually precedes the question.

("A poor, miserable wretch" is Mr. Hsiung's translation for the phrase *suan liu-liu*. Literally it means "something extremely sour to the taste"; hence it can be applied to a person who offends good taste by being too priggishly correct in word or behavior or by being too eager and officious in his attempt to please or impress others.)

The reader of the present translation will not find Scholar Chang's question which prompts Hung Niang's amused observation. This is because Chin Sheng-t'an has deleted much comic dialogue from his version as beneath the dignity of the play. Though Mr. Hsiung has restored a few passages of verse deleted from that edition, his decision to adhere to its prose text is somewhat unfortunate since scholars today would have preferred the earlier Ming editions of Wang's play. When Mr. Hsiung's translation appeared in 1935, however, the prestige of the Chin version, which had prevailed over all other editions during the Ch'ing period, was still very high, and he could not have anticipated the recent change in taste. Though harshly attacked in Communist China for a multitude of sins, Chin Sheng-t'an was of course a critic of some originality, and most Chinese still prefer his truncated, 71-chapter edition of the novel *Shui-hu chuan* (*All Men Are Brothers*, or *The Water Margin*) to the complete 120-chapter edition. In his copious commentary on *Hsi-hsiang chi*, which is in equal portions fatuous and brilliant, he vigorously defends the honor and chastity of Ying-ying, but to maintain his thesis he had to delete much dialogue and several lyrical passages that appeared to him in questionable taste. Thus in the most erotic scene (Part IV, Act 1) the stanza in which Scholar Chang praises the handkerchief stained with Ying-ying's hymenal blood (fortunately restored by

Mr. Hsiung on page 174) has been cut. Chin has also transposed and edited many verse passages and has added dialogue and stage directions of his own devising (all these changes inevitably accompanied by his own ecstatic comments). The slight tampering with several of Hung Niang's stanzas appears to me especially regrettable.

To illustrate Chin Sheng-t'an's bowdlerization of the play, we may examine a small passage in Part III, Act 4. According to the Ming editions, after being rebuffed in the garden by Ying-ying, the lovesick hero soliloquizes as follows:

> My damned (*t'ui*) symptoms cannot be treated by any doctor. If only I could swallow a drop of the young lady's sweet, nice-smelling, cool and dainty saliva, would my damned (*tiao*) sickness be cured.

T'ui and *tiao,* both low terms meaning "penis," are common expletives in Yuan drama. Chin deletes *t'ui* and rewrites the second sentence. In Mr. Hsiung's translation we read accordingly:

> But as my dangerous malady is not one that any skilled doctor can deal with, it is only some good prescription of the Young Lady that can cure it.

As is the case with Shakespearean comedy, the low and erotic language of *Hsi-hsiang chi* in no way diminishes its romantic idealism. On the contrary, in craving for a drop of Ying-ying's saliva, whose restorative properties are defined by a quartet of three-character phrases highly charged with sensuality (only lamely suggested in my translation), Scholar Chang bares his sexual hunger and appears the more sympathetic and passionate as a lover. By not specifying the medicine

he wants, as by toning down his language, the speaker
of the revised passage appears much less impatient
with his desperate condition.

Mr. Hsiung is certainly correct in saying that his
version is "a faithful one" in that he gets the essential
meaning of every verse or prose passage across to the
reader in clear and readable English. But his uniform
language actually does less than adequate justice to the
poetic style of the original, which is at once elegant and
colloquial. Not only is *Hsi-hsiang chi* an adaptation of
Tung's poem but Wang Shih-fu, like all Yuan playwrights, makes a habit of lifting lines and phrases
from earlier poets, especially the *tz'u* poets. At the same
time, however, his arias are unlike *tz'u* poems in their
greater hospitality to colloquial expressions. While
many of these, the so-called *ch'en-tzu*, are added to the
prescribed number of syllables in a given aria and serve
little poetic function beyond imparting a colloquial lilt,
many are an integral part of the aria and they blend
with the more literary phrases to produce lyrical and
dramatic effects not realizable in the *tz'u*.

To a seasoned reader of *Hsi-hsiang chi*, therefore,
it is a steady source of pleasure to spot, on one hand,
the borrowed phrases and lines in juxtaposition to
those of equal lyrical beauty composed by the playwright and, on the other, the more colloquial verses in
a passage of traditional lyrical style. Since his translation is designed for the common reader, we do not expect Mr. Hsiung to identify for us those lines and passages adapted from Tung and other earlier poets;
nevertheless, by judiciously modifying his style, it
would have been possible for him to suggest where the
original verse has produced a decidedly colloquial effect. This, however, Mr. Hsiung has failed to do. Thus,
in Part II, Act 3, vexed with her mother because she is

going to give Scholar Chang only a modest meal, Ying-
ying remarks to Hung Niang, according to Mr. Hsiung:

> Being afraid that I shall cause loss to the family on ac-
> count of my dowry,
> She is showing our gratitude and celebrating my marriage
> by one feast instead of two!

I am afraid that Mr. Hsiung has not quite achieved the
bitter irony of the original not only because his ren-
dition of the second line is debatable (a rare instance
where I would disagree with him) but principally because his genteel style cannot capture the vulgar tone
the heroine has deliberately adopted here in referring
to her forthcoming marriage as a commercial trans-
action financially damaging to her mother. In the first
line she actually says, "She is afraid that I'll be a
p'ei-ch'ien-huo (a thing or article of merchandise which
will cost her plenty to sell or get rid of)." The use of
this colloquial expression implies Ying-ying's utter
contempt for her mother, who is after all a moneyed
dowager.

The arias in *Hsi-hsiang chi* contain a good many
allusions. It is to the credit of Mr. Hsiung that he is
able to provide a highly readable version without re-
sorting to a single footnote. But in the absence of notes
he is often compelled to burden his lines with explana-
tory matter that dilutes the poetry of the original.
Thus in a pair of eight-character lines (Part II, Act
3) Ying-ying uses two allusions to indicate the distance
from her lover newly imposed by her mother. In Mr.
Hsiung's hands these lines swell into 51 words:

> I am suddenly separated from my lover, who may be
> compared with him who was overwhelmed in the
> white waves while keeping his tryst at the Blue
> Bridge,

> Or with him who, missing his beloved, in fury set fire
> to the Temple of the Fire God, which was consumed
> in flames. . . .

The use of footnotes in such cases would have considerably tautened the lines.

At times, Mr. Hsiung shows an apparent distrust of the reader's ability to grasp a metaphor by over-expanding. In Part I, Act 2, for instance, Scholar Chang summarizes Ying-ying's desirability in a memorable four-character phrase, *Juan-yü wen-hsiang* (Soft jade, warm fragrance), which becomes in the present version

> She is as beautiful as jade, but softer to the touch, and as
> fragrant as flowers, but not so cold.

At other times, Mr. Hsiung translates circumspectly, perhaps to avoid embarrassing the reader, as in Part III, Act 3, where Hung Niang sympathizes with Scholar Chang's lovelorn condition:

> I take pity on you, because when you lie down to sleep
> under your coverlet
> You have no one except yourself to comfort you.

In the original the second line, "Your fingers get tired from overwork," refers to masturbation far more explicitly.

I have specified a few types of infelicitous rendering primarily to give the reader an idea of what he will be missing when reading *Hsi-hsiang chi* in the present translation. While I regret that Mr. Hsiung has chosen to use the Chin Sheng-t'an edition as the basic text for his translation, he has, however, done a conscientious job of reproducing in English the paraphrasable meaning of his adopted text in, as he says, a "line for line and sometimes word for word" fashion. Translators

of Chinese verse have despaired of capturing the spirit
and sense of even a four-line poem. How much more
difficult, then, to translate a series of five plays containing stanza after stanza of dramatic verse which retains the elusive weightiness of Chinese lyric poetry!
Mr. Hsiung's *The Romance of the Western Chamber*
has stood well for over thirty years. While we may hope
someday to have a translation which renders the text
of Wang Shih-fu in a more poetic fashion, its reprinting should serve to introduce the ever-increasing number of Western readers of Chinese literature to this
masterpiece of drama.

C. T. HSIA

PREFACE

IN THIS pregnant time of the discussion of international loans and influences, the ancient land of China might reasonably claim that its loan of Mr. S. I. Hsiung to the British theatre should rank among the most important. China's immemorial culture and mansuetude may well have evolved its drama when the European theatre was beginning in Greece; but, however that may be, we have in this volume a faithful reproduction of a highly organized and subtle play that represents the impressive standards set by the Chinese theatre at a time when the naïve simplicities of the nun Hroswitha were symptomatic of the only drama that remained in the Western world. Since then the European theatre has again blossomed marvellously, magnificently in many tongues; then lately, in Britain at any rate, it has shrivelled and ceased to occupy many of drama's most valuable provinces; but through all these ages the Chinese people seems to have been seeing its theatre steadily and seeing it whole, tranquil in the knowledge that, if there is really an immortality of the arts, it is completely operative only when the arts are not subject to fashions and modishness.

Chinese drama, in short, seems to be the only drama that has kept the activities of its theatre whole and complete, as the theatre of Greece was whole and complete; and on this account it has everything to tell to the British theatre that the British theatre most needs to learn—or remember.

Our theatre has not been without workers who have surmised this for a generation; but the beneficent activities of Mr. Hsiung were needed to clarify and make certain his country's message to us.

It is not necessary here to speak of his initial success in introducing his country's drama to Great Britain: *Lady Precious Stream* has been nightly visible in London for nearly a year, and we have never held the gorgeous East in fee more inexpensively or convincingly before, while discerning audiences, in an ecstasy of enjoyment, have learnt from it that many of the essentials of our twentieth-century dramatic method are inessential. At the same time, by parallel writings, Mr. Hsiung has corrected misconceptions regarding the Chinese theatre that had originated in travellers' tales, and has enabled us to understand the important nature of its disregard of actualism.

He also warned us that he was offering us merely a popular melodrama without much pretension to artistic achievement; but he promised that he would follow it, if he received sufficient encouragement, with a version of one of the classics of the Chinese drama that is of classic rank in his country's literature as well.

This volume is the fulfilment of that promise. It is not likely that many of its readers will be in a position to testify to the validity of the translation; but most of those who have had experience of translations of foreign drama will recognize in the directness, clarity, simplicity of Mr. Hsiung's diction and phrasing a guarantee that these virtues are most likely to emanate from understanding and fidelity.

Assuming this, it should be interesting to readers of the present volume to consider a moment why its sponsor should consider it to be a work of a higher class than his first venture. In each of them we have a similar depiction (similar to us, at any rate) of the picturesque side of Chinese life; there are domestic scenes, apparently very much of the same class, military interventions, simple ceremonies of the kind in which the life of the East abounds. Above all, both plays centre about the determination of a Prime Minister's very demure daughter to marry out of her class.

Yet the difference is marked, and especially in the scale of the execution. The economy of diction in the popular melodrama has no place in the classic piece; the latter indeed gives place to long lyric passages which even the abler of our young producer-dictators would characterize as 'literary' and 'undramatic', saying that only heavy cutting could make performance possible. Nevertheless, we know that the piece which contains these passages has held the stage for eight hundred years in China—so that it cannot be undramatic, after all, in a country where the theatre is healthy and whole.

Another fact about these lyric passages is that they are all set down as sung. Without taking Mr. Hsiung's counsel on this point, it is reasonable to assume that the singing in such a performance would bear little or no relation to the processes of vocalization of vowels which are now considered to be singing in Europe, and that the practice indicated by the word is really some stylization of speech (and spoken tone) on defined pitches and cadences—allied in its foundation to the formal element in delivery which is implicit in all utterance of poetry.

Drama here, in fact—in China as in Greece—is relying on expressive sound as part of its method. These lyric and reflective passages can only be characterized as 'undramatic' in an anaemic, feeble theatre that has forgotten what to do with them. They rely, in fact, on that exquisite appropriateness of diction which it is part of our British theatre's business to recapture; and to which China's immemorial living drama can show us the way.

The play is not without its relationships to our European drama. Ying-ying's delicacies are sometimes close to Juliet's; the waiting Chang suffers at one moment almost as the waiting Tristan does. Thought and phrasing evidently touch those of our own great poets once or twice; and such a close as that to Part I is sufficient assurance, by its sudden contrast, that theatric effect in China is closely akin to theatric effect here.

The disposition of the theme in a pentalogy of plays of four short acts each hints at a variety of resource not at present accessible in our theatre; and especially at the freedom which comes to the great dramatist (as in Greece also) when his audience knows all about his subject-matter beforehand as well as he does himself, and novelty and surprise are not required of him. Mr. Hsiung has told us in another connexion that the great plays of the Chinese theatre are not necessarily always performed in their entirety, and that favourite acts are selected to form an infinity of programmes. This, again, presumes a familiarity with traditional themes which is not characteristic of our theatre, but which it well might learn. It also shows our community-drama workers a way in which the delights of this enchanting, delicate, deeply poetic play might be explored gradually and made our own. Such work, and the technical accomplishment it requires, are our theatre's greatest need, and in realizing this we realize how greatly Mr. Hsiung, in helping us to realize it, is our benefactor.

GORDON BOTTOMLEY

THE SHEILING
SILVERDALE
September 1935

WHEN PEOPLE praise the beauty of your wife, no matter how plain you think she is, you cannot help being pleased. On second thoughts, you may suspect them to be either liars or fools, but that would not deprive you of your pleasure. Such is the case with an author and his work. The comments on my first English book made me blush on so many occasions that I decided to publish this volume as soon as I could coax E. V. Rieu to do so, and I hope he will have no cause for regret.

In spite of what I have said, people still refuse to believe that *Lady Precious Stream* is just a popular commercial play—even now after its three-hundredth performance. I said in the very beginning that it was not written for the high-brows—a word so fashionable that I had never heard of it when I was studying English in China—but that it should run. Manager after manager praised its beauty and predicted that it would be an artistic achievement and consequently a commercial failure. I think there is no necessity to call a play an artistic achievement before it has failed financially.

During my struggling days I was told to try some of those producers who are always eager to put on artistic plays which the West End managers have rejected. Try I did, but soon found out what they wanted: plays rejected by other managers, yes! artistic, no! Their sole aim is to produce plays that will run a year or two to show how much cleverer they are than their rivals. As they have much less to choose from, they are naturally much more careful about the commercial possibilities of their choice.

Nowadays managers complain about the scarcity of good plays; but who is to blame?

The Romance of the Western Chamber is really an artistic play, written in the thirteenth century by perhaps two of our great poets. It is generally believed that Wang Shih-fu wrote the first four parts and Kwang Han-ch'ing wrote the Continuation, but some say it is vice versa. And there are people who hold either that Wang or Kwang alone did the complete thing. However, this is quite unimportant with us. In old China a man usually put away his manuscripts and would show them only to his connoisseur-intimates. Works were published only after the death of the author. Royalties were never heard of. When I was speaking of this at a gathering of publishers and authors, the publishers cheered and the authors booed. Although we are uncertain about the authorship of this play, we are unanimous in considering it the masterpiece of poetry and drama. It has held the stage for nearly eight centuries and has enjoyed numerous editions which only the Book of Confucius can rival. Then the latter had been adopted by the authorities as a school text book while the former, on the other hand, was for many years banned. Our elders used to forbid us to read such obscene books, as they called them, but none of them could not recite the complete play!

The theme is based upon a short story written by Yuan Cheng, a poet of the eighth century. Although he tried his best to disguise it, sufficient proof has been found to identify the autobiographical nature of the story. By his poems and later, his biography, we found out this to be his own love affair. One of the Yuan dynasty playwrights faithfully dramatized it and another added, probably at some manager's suggestion, a happy ending. Ever since there have been many pros and cons about this. In Ch'ing dynasty, there was a famous commentator on books, Chin Shên-t'an, who prepared a special complete edition of this play. As he was a man of extremely artistic taste and temperament, he poured endless praises on the first four parts and thrust numerous abuses at the Continuation. The book was overcrowded with margin notes, and some remarks followed every passage. He was very clever and amusing, and had the gift of saying the right thing in the wrong place. When he found any malicious speech by the villain to his liking, he put directly after it: 'Beautiful, excellent; I have never heard anything better than this'; and when he found the poems whispered by the lady to her lover not after his own heart, he would butt in and write between every two lines: 'Rubbish, nonsense; nothing on earth can be worse!'

One thing he did deserves praise. He wrote a very good essay before every act to discuss the incidents which followed. In his comments preceding 'Fulfilment of the Billet-Doux', he severely assaulted those who considered this book as obscene. He said it was a very natural proceeding which had happened in every family ever since the beginning of this world. He further argued that ever since the beginning of this world who could have possibly written such beautiful poetry on such a subject? It gave us a very good excuse when we were caught reading this book in some remote corner.

In translating this play into English, I consulted all the best editions. I followed Chin Shên-t'an's for most of the dialogue and a Ming dynasty edition, annotated by Tz'u Yin-shêng, for the poetry. The hand-written copy by Wen Chêng-ming also helped me with many words and phrases. To translate poetry is extremely difficult. I confess my translation is by no means a good one, but I profess it to be a faithful one. It is a line for line and sometimes word for word translation. I found rhyming would make it necessarily different from the original, and so preferred accuracy to anything else. I realize it is less sinful to write bad books than to translate good books badly, but I hope the good qualities of this book will remain shining in spite of my clumsy English. However, gentle readers, when you find the poetry beautiful, let the merit be attributed to the original authors; and when you find phrases and words unworthy of the name of literature, the translator alone is to blame.

S. I. HSIUNG

LONDON
September 1935

CONTENTS

CONTENTS

PART III

PART IV

CONTINUATION

APPENDIX

ILLUSTRATIONS

xliii

The Romance of the Western Chamber

GENERAL OUTLINE OF THE PLOT

CHANG CHÜN-JUI ingeniously becomes the selected son-in-law of the Eastern Bed.

FA PÊN, the Superior, rules over the Southern Buddhist Monastery.

MADAM TS'UI, the widow of the late Prime Minister, gives a merry feast in the Northern Hall.

TS'UI YING-YING, her daughter, awaits her beloved by moonlight near the Western Chamber.

PART I

THE TITLES OF THE FOUR ACTS OF THE FIRST PART

MADAM TS'UI takes up her quarters in the monastery.
TS'UI YING-YING burns incense at night.
HUNG NIANG, the maid, brings good news.
CHANG CHÜN-JUI upsets the religious ceremony.

ACT I

BEAUTY'S ENCHANTMENT

MADAM TS'UI *enters with* YING-YING, *her daughter*, HUNG NIANG, *the maid, and* HUAN LANG, *the adopted son, and says:*

The surname of my old self is Chêng, the surname of my husband is Ts'ui, and he was the Prime Minister. Unfortunately he fell sick and died, having left behind him only this girl. Her name is Ying-ying, and she is nineteen years old. She is able to sew and embroider, and has other female accomplishments. She can compose poetry, write a good hand, and make calculations with the abacus. When my husband was alive she was betrothed to my nephew, Chêng Hêng, the eldest son of the Minister Chêng. But because the period of mourning has not expired, their marriage has not yet taken place. This little maid has been in the service of my daughter since her childhood, and her name is Hung Niang. This small boy, whose name is Huan Lang, was adopted by my husband so that he might have a descendant. When my husband died, I, with my daughter, wanted to convey his coffin for burial to Po-ling. But we were obstructed on the way, and unable to proceed, so we have arrived at the Ho-chung Prefecture, and have deposited the coffin temporarily in the P'u Chiu Monastery. This monastery, for the encouragement of the performance of good deeds, was erected by the imperial favour of Her Majesty

3

the Empress Wu Tsê Ti'en (A.D. 690–712), whose title was Ti'en Ts'ê Chin Lun. Fa Pên, the Superior, was originally presented for ordination by my husband. On account of this, there is a special building erected to the west of the monastery, in which we are now dwelling. I have also written a letter to the capital requesting Chêng Hêng to come to help us to convey the coffin to Po-ling. When I reflect that while my husband was alive the food spread before us was most sumptuous, and our attendants numbered hundreds, whereas to-day I have only three or four intimate relations with me, I feel very sad!

She sings:

'My husband's official career ended with his life at the Capital.

The widowed mother and the orphaned child while on their journey are in distress.

The coffin, on its way, is reposing in the Buddhist Monastery.

There is no hope of arriving at the old family burial-ground at Po-ling.

The tears of blood which flow from my eyes are as red as the azalea.'

She says:

Now is the time of late spring, which makes one feel rather weary. Hung Niang! look, there is no one at present in the courtyard in front; take your Young Mistress with you and amuse yourselves there for a short time.

HUNG NIANG *says:*

I will do as you bid.

4

YING-YING *sings:*

> 'We have arrived, just as the spring is ending, at the east of the district of P'u.
> Gate after gate of the lonely monastery is firmly barred.
> The flowers, as they fall, redden the flowing stream.
> Innumerable sorrows I bear in silence, but I cannot refrain from
> Resenting the cruel east wind (that has blown down the flowers).'   [*Exeunt.*

MR. CHANG *enters with his* PAGE, *who carries his lute, and says:*

> My surname is Chang, my name is Kung, and I am also styled Chün-jui. My native place is to the west of Lo-yang. My late father was President of the Board of Rites. Having not succeeded in obtaining my official rank, I am travelling about generally. Now is the beginning of the second moon of the seventeenth year of the period Chêng-yüan (A.D. 801). I want to go to the Capital to attend the highest examination. On the way I passed the Ho-chung Prefecture, where I have an old friend. His surname is Tu, his name is Ch'üeh, and he is also styled Chün-shih. He hails from the same district as myself; we were fellow-students, and we have become sworn brothers. Afterwards he abandoned his literary career for a military one, and succeeded in coming out first on the list in the military examination. Then he was appointed *Generalissimo* of the Western Punitive Expedition, and commanded a force of a hundred thousand men. At present he is the military guardian of the P'u Pass. Being in his neighbourhood, I wanted to pay my sworn brother a visit, after which it would not be too late for me to proceed

5

to the capital. I thought to myself that though I had studied by the light of the fire-fly and the reflection of the snow in order to acquire a deep knowledge of literature, I am still a wanderer by lake and sea, and do not yet know when I shall be able to fulfil my great ambition. Mine is truly a case of:

'The sword of very great value lies hidden in the autumn stream,

And black care oppresses the rider on his richly caparisoned steed.'

He sings:

'I travel throughout the empire meeting my literary friends:

With movements as undirected as those of a leaf in the wind.

As I look to the distant horizon, I see the sun which seems nearer than the unseen capital.

Like a bookworm which appears to desire to remain where it is, I have bored my way into the ancient classics

(I have so constantly attended the State examination) that my seat there has not yet had time to cool;

And my inkstone, which is as hard as iron, I have worn out by incessant rubbing.

In order to rise like the roc to the highest region of the clouds,

One must first study more than ten years by the light of snow and the fire-fly.

A highly cultured (person finds it) impossible to adapt himself to the merely vulgar.

When the times are out of joint, a man cannot fulfil his highest aspirations,

6

And cannot be more than a mere poetaster, an engraver
of seals
Or a manipulator of ancient literary fragments.'

He says:

Strolling along, I have arrived at the bank of the
Yellow River. Look, what a magnificent sight it is!

He sings:

'Where exists the special danger from incessant wind
and water?
Surely that is the very spot!
This river passes by the States of Ch'i and Liang,
divides those of Ch'in and Chin and serves as a
defence of Yen.
The foam of the waves, white as snow, reaches the
heavens,
And looks like the autumn clouds that roll in the sky.
The floating bridges, kept together by ropes of bamboo,
Look like black dragons crouching on the waves.
From east to west it passes through nine regions,
And from north to south a hundred streams flow into it.
What does the pace of the home-coming junks recall?
It is like that of an arrow shot from a bow!
The river resembles the Milky Way, tumbling out of
the ninth heaven,
Its source is so high that it seems to be beyond the
clouds.
It maintains its course unchanged until it falls into the
Eastern Sea.
It enriches the many thousand flowers of Lo-yang,
And fertilizes the innumerable acres of Liang Yüan.
Would that I could embark on a raft and sail to the
confines of the sun and moon!'

He says:

> Whilst I have been speaking I have arrived in the
> city, and here is an excellent inn. Lute-bearer,
> hold my horse. Where is the innkeeper?

INNKEEPER *enters, and says:*

> I am the keeper of the inn in the Highest Graduate
> Street. Do you want to stay here, sir? We have
> a very clean room here.

MR. CHANG *says:*

> I will stay in your best room. Innkeeper, come
> here. Is there any place where we can amuse
> ourselves?

INNKEEPER *says:*

> We have the P'u Chiu Monastery here, which was
> erected by the Imperial Order of Her Majesty the
> Empress Wu Tsê Ti'en for the encouragement of
> the performance of good deeds. It is an extra-
> ordinary building, and all those who, from the
> north and south, pass by here never fail to visit it.
> This is the only sight of any interest that we have
> here.

MR. CHANG *says:*

> Lute-bearer, see to my luggage, and unsaddle my
> horse. I am going to visit the monastery.

LUTE-BEARER *says:*

> I will do as you bid.   [*Exeunt.*

FA TS'UNG *enters, and says:*

> I am the priest Fa Ts'ung, and the disciple of Fa
> Pên, the Superior of P'u Chiu Monastery. My
> master has gone abroad to-day to conduct a
> religious ceremony, and has ordered me to remain
> in the monastery to take note of any visitors who

may come, and to inform him on his return. I am now standing at the monastery gate to see if any one is coming.

MR. CHANG *enters, and says:*

'The winding path leads to a beautiful spot,
Where flowers and trees of the monastery abound.'

   Now I have arrived.

      (*They meet.*)

FA TS'UNG *says:*

Where do you come from, sir?

MR. CHANG *says:*

I have come here from the west of Lo-yang. Having heard that your monastery is so very tranquil and beautiful, I have come to worship Buddha, and to pay my respects to your Superior.

FA TS'UNG *says:*

My Superior is not here. I am his disciple, Fa Ts'ung. May I invite you to have a cup of tea in the hall?

MR. CHANG *says:*

Since your Superior is not at home, please don't trouble to give me tea. Will you be so kind as to show me round the monastery?

FA 'Ts'UNG *says:*

Of course, with pleasure.

MR. CHANG *says:*

Indeed, it is a fine building!

He sings:

'With great delight I have seen the Hall of Buddha above,

9

The quarters of the priests below,
The kitchen to the west,
The hall for expounding the law of Buddha to the north,
And the bell-tower in front.
I have wandered through the priests' cells,
Have climbed the pagoda,
And roamed through and through all the passages.
I have counted the number of Arhats,
Worshipped the Buddha,
And made my bow to the sages and saints.'

He says:

There is a fine building. What place is that? Allow me to have the pleasure of visiting it with you.

FA TS'UNG, *stopping him, says:*

You must not go there, so please, sir, remain where you are. Inside is the residence of the family of His Excellency the late Prime Minister Ts'ui.

(MR. CHANG *sees* YING-YING, *who enters with* HUNG NIANG.)

MR. CHANG *sings:*

'I have suddenly observed a beauty, who must be the victim of an amour between us five hundred years old!

Goodness knows how many thousands of beauties I have seen before,
But never have I seen such a delightful maiden as this!
My eyes are bedazzled, and speech fails me,
My soul has soared to mid-heaven!

10

Standing there with her fair shoulders at rest, she seems
    regardless of how admiration of her is expressed,
While she fondles the flower with a smiling face.

Is this a paradise, a heaven where no regrets reign?
Who would have thought that I should meet here such
    an angel,
Who, whether pleased or displeased, is always a vision
    of beauty!
Looking at her profile, most becoming is her emerald
    ornament on her hair.

Her eyebrows, in the imperial style, arched like the
    crescent of the new moon,
Run into the side of her waved locks.
Before she has uttered a word, she blushes at the thought
    of having to speak when others are present.
She opens her lips, red as cherries,
And reveals her teeth, white as jade,
And finally, after some hesitation, she speaks
With a sound like that of the oriole singing amidst the
    flowers.'

YING-YING *says:*
    Hung Niang, I am going to see my mother.

MR. CHANG *sings:*
    'Every step she takes arouses one's affections.
    When she moves, her waist is as graceful and supple as
        that of a dancer,
    With a thousand attractions and ten thousand charms,
    Like the drooping willow in the evening breeze!'

        [*Exeunt* YING-YING *and* HUNG NIANG.

'AMONG THE FALLEN BLOSSOMS ON THE SOFT SWEET-SMELLING PATH

'SHE LEAVES THE SLIGHT IMPRINT OF HER STEPS ON THE FRAGRANT DUST.'

MR. CHANG *sings:*

'Behold, among the fallen blossoms on the soft sweet-
    smelling path,
She leaves the slight imprint of her steps on the fragrant
    dust.

Apart from the love that her glance inspires,
Her gait alone transmits the sentiments of her heart.
Slowly advancing, she arrives at her threshold,
And at that short distance
She purposely turns round to look,
And makes me feel beside myself!
The angel has returned to her paradise,
Leaving behind her only the willows wrapped in mist,
And the chirping of the birds.

Shut is the gate of the remote courtyard where flourish
    the blossoms of the pear trees;
The white wall seems as high as the blue sky.
Hateful is Heaven which opposes the wishes of men!
How can I now pass the time?
How can I linger here?
I am more than in a quandary and know not what to do!

Her fragrance, like that of the lily and the musk, is
    still here,
While the tinkling sound of her jade ornaments becomes
    gradually more remote.
The branches of the weeping willow are tossed by the
    east wind,
And to the gossamer threads, the petals of the flowers
    of the peach tree adhere.
Behind the beaded curtain there seems to be revealed
    her face as brilliant as the hibiscus flower.

While you say this is the residence of the family of the
    Minister at Ho-chung,
I say that it is the temple of the Goddess of Mercy of
    the South Sea!

With gazing, my eyes seem to start out of my head,
And my mouth waters in vain!
Soon this love-sickness will penetrate the very marrow
    of my bones.
How can I bear the bewitching glance she gave when
    she was about to depart!
Were I made even of iron or stone I could not but
    think of her, and adore her.
Around the building the flowers and trees remain the
    same;
The sun in the sky proclaims that it is midday.
The pagoda throws a round shadow.
The beauties of the spring are before my eyes,
But I see not her, who is as beautiful as jade,
And who has converted the Monastery of Buddha into
    a fairyland!'   [*Exeunt*.

ACT II

THE RENTING OF THE QUARTERS IN
THE MONASTERY

MADAM TS'UI *enters with* HUNG NIANG, *and says:*

Hung Niang, take the following message for me. Ask the Superior of the monastery when it will suit him to perform the religious service for my late husband. When he has told you, come back and report to me.

HUNG NIANG *says:*

I will do as you bid.   [*Exeunt.*

FA PÊN *enters, and says:*

I am the priest Fa Pên, the Superior of this P'u Chiu Monastery. Last night I went to perform a religious ceremony in a village. I wonder whether any one has been here to visit me.

(*He summons* FA TS'UNG *to inquire.*)

FA TS'UNG *enters, and says:*

Last night a graduate from the west of Lo-yang came here on purpose to visit you, my master; but having failed to meet you he went away.

FA PÊN *says:*

Go and keep watch outside the monastery gate, and if he comes back again let me know.

FA TS'UNG *says:*

I will do as you bid.

MR. CHANG *enters, and says:*

> Since I saw that young lady yesterday evening I have remained awake all night. To-day I have come again to the monastery to call upon the Superior, to whom I have something particular to say.

> (*He makes his bow to* FA TS'UNG.)

He sings:

> 'If you don't show mercy by helping to promote my interest,
> I will never forgive you, Priest Fa Ts'ung.'

FA TS'UNG *says:*

> So you have come, sir. I don't understand what you say.

MR. CHANG *sings:*

> 'I want you to let me have half a guest-room or a cell,
> So that I may live opposite the door of the quarters of her whom I love to distraction.
> Although I cannot steal the heart of this ravishing beauty,
> I can at least enjoy the sight of her movements, beautiful as those of the clouds, and the mutual exchange of glances.'

FA TS'UNG *says:*

> I do not understand what you say, sir.

MR. CHANG *sings:*

> 'Formerly, when I saw a painted face, I truly thought it to be shameful,
> And painted eyebrows I regarded as misleading artifice.
> But now that I, indifferent though I am, see this lovely lady
> My heart is full of a loving desire,

17

Which bewilders my mind,
Dazzles my sight,
And creates a whirling sensation within me.'

FA TS'UNG *says:*

> I still do not understand what you say, sir. My master has been waiting for a long time. I will go to inform him.
>
> (MR. CHANG *meets* FA PÊN.)

MR. CHANG *sings:*

'I see before me one whose head is like snow,
His locks like frost,
And whose appearance is like that of a youth, owing to his knowing the secret of how to preserve his health.
His presence is nobly impressive,
His voice is clear and strong;
Had he but a halo
He would be the very image of the Buddha!'

FA PÊN *says:*

> Please come and take a seat inside the hall, sir. Last night I was not at home, so I failed to welcome you. I hope you will forgive me.

MR. CHANG *says:*

> I have for long heard of your high reputation, and wished to come and hear you preach. But, un-expectedly, I missed you yesterday. Now that I have met you, I feel that I have had, am having, and will have good fortune in my three existences.

FA PÊN *says:*

> May I ask you, sir, where your family comes from, your honourable surname, and your fine name, and why you have come here?

18

MR. CHANG *says:*

> I am a native of the west of Lo-yang; my surname is Chang, my name is Kung, and I am also styled Chün-jui; I am passing through here on my way to the highest examination in the Capital.

He sings:

'The great Master has minutely questioned me about my movements.

I will open to him my heart in full detail:

I come from the west of Lo-yang, which is my native home,

My forebears were officials in various parts of the empire,

And settled for some time at Hsien-yang.

My late father, who was President of the Board of Rites, enjoyed a great fame;

He died of sickness when over fifty years of age.

During the whole of his life he was just and upright and free from prejudice,

With the result that he left behind him nothing but an empty purse.

I have heard that you, with all your brilliant qualities, know how to condescend to those in a humbler sphere;

And truly you appear to me as pure as the wind, and as bright as the moon.

I no longer wish to seek office.

My sole desire is to hear your instructions.'

He says:

> As I am now travelling, I have no means of showing my respect for you, but may I venture to offer an ounce of silver for the general expenses of the

monastery, with the hope that you will kindly accept it.

He sings:

'A graduate's presents have ever been as light as half a sheet of paper;

He is quite ignorant of the real value of money;

He cares not whether men discuss his failings or his merits;

He has no fear of his conduct being weighed and minutely examined.

I have specially come to pay a visit.

You must really not refuse my small gift.

That trifle is neither sufficient to buy firewood nor to purchase food for the monastery.

At best, it is only enough to provide some tea or soup.

If you will undertake to speak a word for me to that beauty,

Living or dead, I will never forget you.'

FA PÊN *says:*

Why, sir, do you act in this way when you are travelling? You must have something to tell me, sir.

MR. CHANG *says:*

I venture to make a request. I dislike the inn because it is so crowded that I cannot study the classics and the histories. I therefore wish to rent for a time a room here, so that, morning and evening, I may be able to hear your teaching. As for the monthly rent of the room, I will pay what you wish.

FA PÊN *says:*

There are quite a number of empty rooms in our

monastery. You can choose which you want. Or, if you like, you can share my couch with me. What do you say?

MR. CHANG *sings:*

'I do not want the chamber where incense is stored,
Nor the antiquated wooden hall;
I want no room to the south,
Nor to the east;
But a room near the Western Chamber, where the main
    passage runs by the ante-room.
That is the place after my heart!
Please do not mention at all the cell where the Superior
    dwells!'

HUNG NIANG *enters, and says:*

My Mistress has ordered me to inquire from the Superior when it will suit him to perform the religious service for my late master, and when he has told me, to return and report to her.

(*She meets* FA PÊN.)

Ten thousand blessings, Superior! My Mistress has sent me to inquire when it will suit you to perform the religious service for my late master.

MR. CHANG *says:*

What a pretty girl!

He sings:

'Her dignified and correct manners reveal her as having
    associated with a noble family;
She does not show the slightest sign of coquetry;
Having made a deep curtsy to the great Superior,
She opens her red lips and speaks with perfect pro-
    priety.

21

Her delightful face is only slightly coloured,
And she is dressed in a mourning raiment of pure white.
With unusual and intelligent eyes like those of a bird,
She steals a look, but her eyes show no regard for
  Mr. Chang.
If I could share the couch of your Young Mistress,
I would not even trouble you to make the bed for us,
But I will ask your Young Mistress and her mother to
  give you your freedom;
But should they not grant it,
I would myself write a deed allowing you to marry a
  good husband!'

FA PÊN *says:*

> Will you take a seat for a moment, sir, while I go
> with the young maid to see the Hall of Buddha?
> I will return at once.

MR. CHANG *says:*

> What do you say to my accompanying you?

FA PÊN *says:*

> By all means.

MR. CHANG *says:*

> Let the young maid go in front, and I will keep a
> respectful distance behind.

He sings:

'Attractively arrayed is the maid of the Ts'ui family,
It may be that she is displaying her charms before the
  old ascetic monk.
If she is not glancing coquettishly at you,
Then why is she in such particularly beautiful array?

In these passages and the chambers of the monastery,
Your good fortune from heaven awaits you!'

22

FA PÊN *angrily says:*

> What are you with your fine airs talking about there?

MR. CHANG *says:*

> You must not blame me for what I cannot help saying.

He sings:

'My rude and foolish assumption of fine airs
Has offended and angered the holy Superior.
But is such a great family without any male servant
That it must send a maid as its messenger?
If you insist upon having your own say,
Then you must look out for your own skin!'

FA PÊN *says:*

> It is because the daughter of the late Prime Minister Ts'ui, prompted by her filial feelings for her late father, wishes to hold a religious service, thoroughly sincere and earnest, and not wishing to send any other person, she has dispatched her own personal maid, Hung Niang, to inquire about the date of the service.

He turns, and says to HUNG NIANG:

> The offerings and other preparations for the religious service are all complete. The fifteenth day of the moon is the day on which the Buddha receives offerings, so I request Madam Ts'ui and her daughter to come on that day to offer incense.

MR. CHANG, *dissolved in tears, says:*

'Alas! Alas! My father and my mother!
What pain and toil my birth gave you!
I long to repay your great kindness,
Which is like great Heaven, illimitable!'

The young lady, though a girl, still desires to show her gratitude to her father. I hope, therefore, that out of your kindness and mercy you will allow me to subscribe five thousand cash, so that I may be included somehow in a service for the saving of the souls of my deceased parents, and thereby fulfil my duty as a son. I feel pretty sure that when Madam Ts'ui knows my wish she will not raise any objection.

FA PÊN *says:*

Of course not! Fa Ts'ung, arrange to include Mr. Chang in the service accordingly.

MR. CHANG *privately asks* FA TS'UNG:

Is the Young Lady sure to be present?

FA TS'UNG *says:*

How could she possibly not be present, seeing that the service is for her own father?

MR. CHANG *joyfully says:*

I have indeed made a good use of those five thousand cash!

He sings:

'The sight of Ying-ying, either in Heaven or on Earth,
Is better than all the sacrifices ever offered!
She is as beautiful as jade, but softer to the touch, and
as fragrant as flowers, but not so cold.
Not to speak of the joy of embracing her,
The mere touch of her
Would be sufficient to dispel at once all trouble and
misfortune!'

FA PÊN *says:*

Let us all go to the hall to have tea.

24

MR. CHANG *says:*

> Please excuse me for a moment.

Moving to a certain spot, he says:

> I will wait for the maid; she is sure to come here.

HUNG NIANG, *bidding farewell to* FA PÊN, *says:*

> I must not take any tea for fear my Mistress will wonder what is delaying me. I am going to report to her.   [*She departs.*

MR. CHANG, *meeting her with a salute, says:*

> I make my bow to you, fair maid!

HUNG NIANG *says:*

> Ten thousand blessings, sir!

MR. CHANG *says:*

> Are you not Hung Niang, the personal maid of the Young Lady, Ying-ying?

HUNG NIANG *says:*

> I am! Why do you trouble to ask me?

MR. CHANG *says:*

> If I may be allowed, I have something to say to you.

HUNG NIANG *says:*

> 'Words, like arrows,
> Must not be uttered at random;
> For once they enter the human ear,
> They cannot be forcibly removed!'
>
> If you have something to say, however, don't be afraid to speak.

MR. CHANG *says:*

> My surname is Chang, my name is Kung, and I am also styled Chün-jui. My native place is to

25

the west of Lo-yang. I am twenty-three years of age. I was born on the seventeenth day of the first moon, at the hour of the Rat. I am still unmarried.

HUNG NIANG *says:*

Who asked you all these? I am not a fortune-teller who wants to know such particulars, so what is the good of telling me the year, the moon, and the day of your birth?

MR. CHANG *says:*

I have still a question to ask you: Is your Young Mistress in the habit of going abroad?

HUNG NIANG *says:*

What has her going abroad to do with you? You are an educated gentleman; don't you know what Confucius said: 'Speak not what is contrary to propriety, and make no movement which is contrary to propriety!' My Mistress rules her family strictly and sternly, and is cold as ice and frost. Even a mere boy dares not enter her middle chamber unless he has been summoned. How can you, who are in no way connected with the family, behave like this? Fortunately it is I in whose presence you have spoken, and who can pardon you. If my Mistress knew what you had asked, how could the matter end here? In future, ask only what is proper to ask, and don't be bold enough to ask what you shouldn't ask.   [*Exit.*

MR. CHANG, *after a long pause, says:*

This love-sickness will surely be the death of me.

He sings:

'Having heard what she said, I feel sad and distressed in heart;

My overwhelming grief is shown in my knitted eyebrows.

She said that the cold purity of her Mistress is like that
of the ice and frost;

And that no one, unless summoned, can enter the
middle chamber.

I reflect, that if you, her daughter, stand in such awe
of your strict and stern mother,

It was wrong to turn round to look at me just before
you departed.

If I have to give you up, tell me how I can,

While the image of you is engraved on my soul and
imprinted on my whole being?

If in this life we are not to be joined together as twin
lilies,

Can it be that I, in a previous existence, prayed that all
relations between us should end?

But my real desire is to hold you in my embrace as my
special precious one,

And to keep my love for you for ever warm in my heart
of hearts

While worshipping your image with my eyes.

I have always heard that the Wu Mountain (where
lovers meet) is as remote as Heaven,

But our place of meeting seems even more remote than
the Wu Mountain.

Though I stand here in the flesh in this passage,

My soul is not here, but with her.

Perhaps she is ready to tell the feelings of her heart to
her lonely lover.

But her fear is that her sentiments may be revealed to
her stern parent.

27

When she sees the orioles and butterflies flying in pairs,
    her heart aflame with love is moved.

Hung Niang, young and obstinate you are!
Could I only but hold her in my embrace
She would at first sight regard me as all her fancy
    painted,
While I would regard her as the sweetest girl that ever
    lived.
Such an enravishing meeting
Might result in my becoming the beloved husband,
And what would she care for the strict control of a
    mother!

Hung Niang, you are over-anxious, and your forecast
    of the future is vain.
When a fine young man has met a charming lady, and
    they are both of a suitable age,
He is bound to think of the happy time when, as his
    wife, he will be painting her eyebrows like Chang
    Ch'ang of old.
And she is sure to think of the happy time when he will
    be her husband, as in the story of Yüan.
I am not exaggerating when I say
She is perfect in virtue, in speech, in accomplishments,
    and in looks,
And her lover is courteous, temperate, benign, and
    upright.

Hung Niang, the eyebrows of your Young Mistress are
    delicately traced,
And her cheeks are only slightly tinted.
Her neck is as smooth as jade, and as white as if
    sprinkled with fragrant powder.

28

She is arrayed in a skirt of green, embroidered with love-birds, revealing feet as beautiful as golden lilies.

And her red sleeves are embroidered with phoenixes, disclosing fingers as delicate and white as shoots of bamboo.

Could I banish you from my thoughts it would indeed be better for me!

If you could only remove your overwhelming attractions,

Then I would be freed from the many thoughts which perplex me.'

He says:

I forgot to say good-bye to the Superior.

Turning round and meeting FA PÊN, *he says:*

May I venture to ask you about the rooms?

FA PÊN *says:*

There is a room adjoining the Western Chamber; it is very delightful and charming, and quite suitable for you. You may occupy it at your convenience, sir.

MR. CHANG *says:*

I will now return to the inn to bring my luggage here.

FA PÊN *says:*

Be sure to come back, sir.

[*Exeunt* FA PÊN *and* FA TS'UNG.

MR. CHANG *says:*

The luggage is easy to remove, but how can I endure my loneliness?

29

He sings:

'Hung Niang, I am all alone in my deserted chamber
    and my mat and pillow are as cold as ice;
My solitary lamp throws a fitful shadow on my book.
Even if I fulfil my ambition in this life,
How can I endure the sufferings of this night that seems
    never to end?
Sleepless, I roll from side to side,
At least, I have heaved ten thousand deep sighs and
    short groans,
And I have five thousand times beaten my pillow and
    hammered my bed!

She is bashful and beautiful, and more lovely than a
    flower, for she can understand human speech,
And her skin is as delicate and smooth as jade with a
    rare fragrance.
Having met her so hurriedly, it is difficult to remember
    distinctly her charming form.
Unable to sleep, I rest my hand on my cheek and am
    full of thoughts of her whom I love.'   [*Exit.*

ACT III

A POEM AND ITS RESPONSE

YING-YING *enters, and says:*

> My mother has sent Hung Niang to inquire from the Superior on what day he will perform the religious service. She has been absent for a long time without coming back to report.

HUNG NIANG *enters, and says:*

> I have already reported to my Mistress. I must now go and tell my Young Mistress.

YING-YING *says:*

> You were sent to inquire when the Superior would perform the religious service.

HUNG NIANG *says:*

> I have just made a report to my Mistress, and now I want to report to you. The fifteenth of the second moon is the date on which is offered goodness knows what sacrifice to Buddha, and the Superior requests you and your mother to burn incense on that date. (*Laughing*, HUNG NIANG *says:*) My Young Mistress, I have a very amusing adventure to tell you. The graduate we met the other day when we were in the courtyard of the monastery, was to-day sitting in the hall. He went out in advance to wait for me, and, making a deep bow to me, said: 'Are you not Hung Niang, the personal maid of the young lady, Ying-ying?' and

went on to say: 'My surname is Chang, my name is Kung, and I am also styled Chün-jui. My native place is to the west of Lo-yang. I am twenty-three years of age. I was born on the seventeenth day of the first moon at the hour of the Rat. I am still unmarried.'

YING-YING *says:*

Who told you to question him?

HUNG NIANG *says:*

Yes, indeed, who? He also mentioned your name, and asked if you are in the habit of going abroad. But I gave him a good scolding before I left to return.

YING-YING *says:*

It would be as well if you had not scolded him.

HUNG NIANG *says:*

I don't know what on earth he is thinking about. When there is such a fool in existence, why shouldn't I scold him?

YING-YING *says:*

Have you told my mother about it or not?

HUNG NIANG *says:*

No, I have not said a word about it to her.

YING-YING *says:*

You must never breathe a word about it in future to her. It is getting late; arrange the table for the incense-burner, and we will go into the garden to burn incense.

'Oh! How unexpected love affects my heart,
When I, leaning against the brazier, am purposelessly
    watching the moon!'   [*Exeunt.*

MR. CHANG *enters, and says:*

> I have moved to the monastery and have actually occupied rooms near the Western Chamber. I now know, by inquiring from the priest, that the young lady burns incense every night in the garden. Fortunately the garden is only separated from my quarters by a wall; so that, when she comes out, I can await her by the rocks near the corner of the wall, and feast my eyes on her. What could be better than that! Happily, it is now midnight, and there is no one about; the moon is shining, the air is clear, a truly delightful time!

'When I am at leisure I can visit the priest in his hall,
And when I am sad I can hum my poem in the bright
moonlight in front of the Western Chamber.'

He sings:

'In the clear sky, there is not a speck of cloud;
The Silver River casts its gentle light;
The moon shines brightly in the sky,
And the shadows of the flowers fill the courtyard.
When through her sleeves of silk she feels the cold,
Her tender heart will surely realize the time is late.
I incline my ear and listen;
I walk softly along;
Silently and furtively so as not to be seen, I await her.

I await that perfect, charming, and graceful maiden
Ying-ying.
After the first watch the world is wrapped in silence.
I will go straight to the courtyard of Ying-ying,
And, arrived at the passage there, I will confront you
unexpectedly—you, whom I love to distraction—
And make sure of holding you firmly in my embrace,

And ask you to tell me why our meetings are so short,
while our partings are so long
That it seems as if it were only your shadow and not
your fair image that you have left behind.'

YING-YING *enters with* HUNG NIANG, *and says:*

Open the side door, and take out the table for the
incense-burner.

MR. CHANG *sings:*

'I suddenly hear the creaking of the side door,
As the wind passes by it carries to me the delicate
fragrance of her raiment;
On tiptoe I intently fix my gaze on her;
She appears even more beautiful than when I first saw
her.
Now that to-night I am really able to see her charms,
I find that she outvies, in the beauty of her carriage,
the Goddess of the Moon.'

He says:

I imagine that this beauty, disliking convention,
has availed herself of the opportunity to escape
from her confined surroundings, and has revealed
to me her fair face and charming person. She
stands there in silence and without movement, with
her long sleeves and her silk skirt hanging down.
She is like the fair lady Hsiang Ling, leaning
against the red door of the temple of the Emperor
Shun, and like the Nymph of the Lo River, who
wished to have her love for the Prince of Ch'ên
described in verse. Truly a beauty is she!

He sings:

'Haltingly she wends her way along the fragrant path.
Maybe her small feet find progress difficult.

34

As she approaches nearer, her numerous attractions are
  more clearly seen,
And how can I prevent them from taking possession of
  my soul?'

YING-YING *says:*

Bring the incense here.

MR. CHANG *says:*

I would like to hear the Young Lady's prayers.

YING-YING *says:*

In burning this first stick of incense, I pray that
my deceased father may soon ascend to Heaven.
In burning this, the second, I pray that my dear
mother may live for a hundred years. As to this,
the third . . . (*She hesitates for some time.*)

HUNG NIANG *says:*

Why is it that you are always silent when it comes
to the third? Let your maid Hung Niang pray
for her Mistress. I pray that my Young Mistress
may marry a husband whose literary talents are
second to none, and who may come out first in his
grand literary examination, who is a fine cavalier,
who has a gentle disposition, and who may be
spared to live with my Young Mistress for a
hundred years.

YING-YING *puts the third stick into the burner, and kneels:*

'*All the sorrows of her heart*
Were comprehended in that last act of most sincere
worship.'
    (*She heaves a deep sigh.*)

MR. CHANG *says:*

What is there in your heart that makes you sigh so
deeply as you lean on the balustrade?

He sings:

> 'The night is late, the clouds of incense float in the air
> of the courtyard,
> The curtains are unmoved by the east wind.
> Her worship ended, she leans on the balustrade of the
> winding passage
> And heaves more than one deep sigh.
> The bright full moon shines like a round mirror in the
> clear sky,
> From which all clouds and mists are absent.
> All that is visible is the smoke of the incense and the
> vapour from mortal mouths.
> But which is smoke, and which is vapour cannot be
> distinguished.'

He says:

> After careful consideration, I think that the Young
> Lady's sigh must arise from some feelings of her
> heart. Although I cannot compare with Ssŭ-ma
> Hsiang-ju, you are indeed another Wên-chün!
> Let me try to compose a poem and read it to her,
> and see what she will say.
>
> 'This is a beautiful moonlight night,
> And the shadows of the flowers quietly fall.
> Why do we, who are in the pure light of the moon,
> See not the goddess who dwells there?'

YING-YING *says:*

> There is some one, at the corner of the wall, who
> is chanting a poem.

HUNG NIANG *says:*

> The sound of the voice is exactly that of that
> foolish fellow who is twenty-three years old and
> still unmarried.

YING-YING *says:*

>What a pure and fresh poem! Hung Niang, I will compose one to rhyme with his.

HUNG NIANG *says:*

>Yes, do try to compose one, and let me hear it.

YING-YING *reads:*

'In my boudoir, profound solitude reigns,
Without purpose the sweet time of my youth is passing
 away!
I think the poet whose verses I have just heard
Will take pity on her who sighed so deeply.'

MR. CHANG, *surprised and overjoyed, says:*

>How very promptly she has responded to my verses!

He sings:

'Her face, so full of charms, has already driven me to
 distraction,
But, what is more, in her mind there lies deep wisdom.
She has responded to my impromptu verses so aptly,
Every word has revealed her feelings,
And is pleasant to hear.
Soft are her words,
And pure are her rhymes.
Justly are you named the Singing Oriole.
If you would but look at me without turning away,
Then we could carry on our rhyming till daybreak with
 the wall between us,
And there indeed would be a case of true understanding.'

He says:

>I must get to the other side of the wall, to see what the Young Lady will do.

He sings:

'I would like to tuck up my silk robe and go to see her,
Who might welcome me with a smiling face.
Hung Niang, hitherto so unkind to me, you must not
    make light of my love for your Young Mistress.
You should persuade her that she should graciously
    comply with my desire.

But suddenly I hear a sound which startles me!'

HUNG NIANG *says:*

We ought to go in, or else the Mistress will be
displeased and scold us.

[*Exeunt* YING-YING *and* HUNG NIANG,
shutting the side door.

MR. CHANG *sings:*

'At the sound, the birds, which were asleep, fly up with
    fluttering wings,
And the whole path is covered with red blossoms that
    have fallen.

The dew, glistening on the pure green moss, lies cold.
The shadow of the brilliant moonlight is sifted through
    the flowers.
By day, my thoughts are ever of you, though my love-
    sickness is vain;
But to-night I will find the real cure for that sickness.

Your curtains are drawn,
And your doors are closed.
When I ventured to whisper a question to you,
You, in low tone, have replied.
When the moon was bright, and the wind was pure,
And it was just the hour of the second watch,
That ought to have been our opportunity.

But now, you seem not destined to be my love,
While I am the victim of cruel Fate.

As I am finding my way back, I hesitate and pause for
   a moment.
The branches of bamboo are rocked in the wind,
And the Dipper and the Bushel have moved their
   positions in the sky.
Oh! to-night though I am miserable, there are yet some
   good signs.
If she cares not for me, for whom then does she care?
There is no need for her beautiful eyes to show her love,
For I know that she loves me though she speaks not.'

He says:

   But to-night, how can I persuade the Spirit of
   Sleep to visit my eyes?

He sings:

'My lamp on its low stand sheds an inconstant blue
   flame,
My old screen seems cold and lonely.
My lamp is dim,
And I dream not of her!
Bitter is the wind that comes through the latticed
   windows;
It makes the paper that covers the windows rattle!
My pillow is solitary,
And my coverlet is lonely.
Even a man of iron would feel emotion!

I can neither hate nor complain;
I can neither sit up nor find sleep!
Some day, under the shelter of the willow and the
   shadow of the flowers,

39

Screened by the mist and surrounded by the clouds,
When night is far advanced, and no one is abroad,
With the sea and hills as witnesses to our oath and troth,
We will rejoice in the enjoyment of our love.
Our future will be a primrose path,
Full of tenderness and love,
And our affection for each other will naturally increase
    more and more in our adorned home!

To-night all my good fortune has been definitely
    established.
My poem and her response are clear evidence of this.
No longer need I seek her green, locked chamber in my
    dreams.
All I need is to await my love beneath the flowering
    peach tree!'   [*Exit.*

ACT IV

THE INTERRUPTION OF THE RELIGIOUS SERVICE

MR. CHANG *enters, and says:*

> To-day is the fifteenth of the second moon, and the priest has requested me to join in the service by burning incense, so I must go along,

> 'Gently and smoothly, like the still clouds and falling rain, pours forth the eloquence of the preacher,
> Rapidly and lightly, like the rolling waves and mild breeze, they turn over the palm leaves of the scriptures.'

He sings:

> 'The full moon shines high above the Monastery of Buddha.
> Streams of auspicious smoke of the incense enwreathe the green-tiled roof.'

FA PÊN *enters with all the other priests, and says:*

> To-day is the fifteenth day of the second moon. It is the day on which Sâkyamuni entered Nirvana, and the day on which Bodhisattva Mañdjusrî and Auysman Çunda made offerings to Buddha. Those who are religious, both male and female, and who to-day perform a religious service, are sure to secure great happiness and advantage. Mr. Chang has already arrived. All of you priests can now play your sacred instruments. When dawn comes,

41

I will request Madam and her daughter to come to burn incense.

MR. CHANG *sings:*

'The smouldering of the incense creates a dense cloud,
The repeating of the prayers is like the sound of sea-
    waves,
The banners throw their shadows as they undulate to
    and fro,
All the benefactors of the monastery have arrived.

The sound of the sacred drums and the brazen cymbals
Is like the thunder in the second moon of spring,
    permeating every corner of the monastery.
The ringing of the bell, and the invocation to Buddha
Are like a sudden storm of wind and rain among the
    pine trees.
The priests are not permitted to knock at the door of
    the quarters where the late Minister's family lives,
Hung Niang, the maid, has not yet reported that the
    lady in the boudoir is coming.
I am all aflame with the hungry desire to see her,
And when I do see her I never will avert my gaze!'

FA PÊN *sees* MR. CHANG, *and says:*

You make your offering first. If Madam Ts'ui
asks you, you must simply say that you are a
relation of mine.

MR. CHANG *burns the incense and prays:*

'May all who are alive enjoy long life on earth!
May those who have passed away be happy in Paradise!
For the sake of the souls of my parents, I sincerely
    worship the "Three Holies".

Again I burn incense and secretly pray:
That Hung Niang, the maid, may not prove my enemy;
That Madam may not discover my love,
And that the dog may not bark.
Pray, oh, Buddha! lend your aid to our secret assignation!'

MADAM *enters with* YING-YING *and* HUNG NIANG, *and says:*

We are now going to burn the incense as requested by the Superior.

MR. CHANG *sings:*

'She seemed to be a fair angel from the blue sky,
But she is actually a lovely maiden coming to offer worship.
But how can I, a sad and lovesick swain,
Resist such overwhelming beauty as she possesses?

Behold that mouth, with cherry-red lips, exhaling fragrance!
Her nose in colour is like the purest jade!
Delicately white as the flower of the pear tree is her face!
Lissom as the willow is her graceful figure!
Charming indeed is she, with a face that is entirely bewitching!
Lithe in her movements, she is complete in her charms.'

FA PÊN *says:*

I have something to tell you, madam: a relation of mine, who is a graduate, is on his way to the Capital. After the death of his parents he could find no way to show his gratitude to them, so he has asked me to include him in this religious service. I promised that I would, but I fear that I may have incurred your displeasure.

43

MADAM *says:*

> How could you incur my displeasure, seeing that
> he desires to join in the service in order to show
> his gratitude to his parents? Please ask him to
> come and see me.

(MR. CHANG *meets* MADAM.)

MR. CHANG *sings:*

> 'The Superior, although advanced in years,
> From his high seat, keeps his eyes fixed on the fair lady.
> The head monk, who reads out the list, has indeed
>   become a fool,
> For he is striking the head of Fa Ts'ung instead of the
>   bell!
> The old and young, ugly and pretty, are all mixed
>   together, in greater confusion than that of the
>   New Year celebration!
> She is, indeed, a perfect beauty such as my heart desires.
> Afraid that she may be seen looking at others,
> She casts a sly glance from her eyes full of tears.
>
> She fills my heart with a longing that cannot be realized.
> She is weeping, and the sound is like that of an oriole
>   on a tree in a forest.
> Her tears are like the pearly dew on the flower.
> It is impossible to follow the example of the Superior,
> Who hides his kindly face with his sleeve.
> Provoking is the acolyte who lights the candles;
> Annoying is the priest who is burning the incense;
> The red light of the candles flickers,
> The smoke of the incense rises in clouds;
> Through their looking at Ying-ying so intently,
> The candles go out and the incense ceases to burn!'

44

YING-YING *says to* HUNG NIANG:

That student has been fussing all night.

She sings:

'In appearance he looks gallant, being in the prime of
his youth;
In nature he must be clever, with a knowledge un-
equalled in this world.
Swaying his body he makes a hundred gestures;
Pacing to and fro before the crowd he displays his
graces.
In the evening, as well as in the daytime,
He makes a great fuss outside the window.
In his library, when he is about to go to bed,
He is sure to heave a thousand deep sighs,
So how can he spend the night in peace?'

MR. CHANG *sings:*

'My love for her is revealed even at the point of my
eyebrows,
She knows well the feelings of my heart;
The sorrow which springs from her heart
Is due to a love which I can guess.
Filled with sorrow and despair,
I hear the sound of the striking of the hanging gong,
The loud tones of the priests and the novices reciting
their scriptures;
Loud though your tones may be, you should not attempt
to rob one of her whom I love.

To love is worse than not to love!
As I, who have loved profoundly without response,
know to my sad cost.'

FA PÊN, *reciting the prayers for the service and burning paper money, says:*

> The dawn has come; I request you, Madam, and your daughter to return to your quarters.

[*Exeunt* MADAM, YING-YING, *and* HUNG NIANG.

MR. CHANG *says:*

> Another day like this would be a joy indeed!   What am I to do now?

He sings:

> 'A busy night we have spent!
> The moon has already disappeared.
> The bell has already sounded.
> The cock has already crowed.
> The fair lady has already departed quickly.
> The religious service has already ended.
> The place of worship has been deserted.
> All the worshippers have gone home in the dark,
> And dawn creeps in a little too soon!'   [*Exeunt.*

PART II

THE TITLES OF THE FOUR ACTS OF THE SECOND PART

CHANG CHÜN-JUI relieves the monastery from the attack of the bandits.

HUNG NIANG, the maid, invites the guest.

MADAM TS'UI goes back on her promise about the marriage.

TS'UI YING-YING listens to the lute at night.

ACT I

THE ALARM AT THE MONASTERY

Sun, *the* Flying Tiger, *enters with a company of soldiers and says:*

I am Sun, the Flying Tiger. At present the
Empire is in a state of disorder. My Commander-
in-Chief, Ting Wên-ya, has been discharging his
duties in an irregular manner. I have been given
a separate command of five thousand soldiers,
including cavalry, to guard Ho-Ch'iao. I have
ascertained that Ying-ying, the daughter of the
late Prime Minister, Ts'ui Chüeh, has black eyebrows with a winning expression, a face as beautiful as the lotus in spring, and is of such overwhelming charm as makes her the peer of the most
famous beauties of old. She is now in the P'u Chiu
Monastery, where the coffin of her late father is
resting, and where she is at present living. On the
fifteenth of the second moon a religious service was
held in memory of her father, at which many
people saw her. When I reflect that even my chief
is irregular in his conduct, why should I not follow
his example? Officers and soldiers, listen to my
command! All you men, with your mouths
gagged, and the horses bitted, march all night long
to the Prefecture of Ho-chung, and forcibly capture Ying-ying to be my wife. Then the desire of
my life will be completely fulfilled!

[*Exit with his troops.*

FA PÊN, *entering in great agitation, says:*

> A calamity has come upon us! Who would have
> thought that Sun, the Flying Tiger, would have
> led five thousand bandit soldiers to surround the
> gates of the monastery as tightly as iron hoops
> round a barrel? They are sounding gongs, beating
> drums, loudly shouting, and waving flags. They
> want to kidnap the Young Lady and make her the
> Flying Tiger's wife. I dare not try to hush up
> the matter, but must at once inform Madam and
> her daughter.

MADAM, *entering in great agitation, says:*

> What on earth is to be done? What on earth is to
> be done? Superior, you and I must go to discuss
> the matter outside my daughter's room.

> [*Exeunt.*

YING-YING *enters with* HUNG NIANG, *and says:*

> When I saw Mr. Chang the other day at the
> religious service I was so beside myself that I
> could scarcely eat or drink; and my feelings were
> intensified by the fact that the air of late spring
> inspired me with love. True, indeed, is the
> sentiment:

'The pure moon fills with pity those who are in love;
  Innumerable sorrows I bear in silence, but I
  cannot refrain from resenting the east wind that
  has blown down the flowers.'

YING-YING *sings:*

'My many sorrows are gradually wearing me away,
And now spring, the romantic time of the year, is nearly
    over.
My robe of silk fits me no longer,

And how many nights of loneliness like this can I
   endure?
All I can do is not to roll up my curtains while the
   fragrant mist is being wafted by the wind,
And to keep the door firmly closed while the pear tree
   blossoms are being scattered by the rain,
And to remain no longer on the balcony in contempla-
   tion of the distant marching clouds.

The red blossoms have fallen in hosts;
And thousands of petals, twirled in the wind, make
   me sad.
Last night my dreams were about beautiful poetry of
   spring,
And this morning on my balcony I bade farewell to the
   season.
The butterflies and the willow catkins, intermingled,
   are like a snow scene.
The soil from the fallen flowers has been made into the
   nest of the swallow.
Alas! that my affection for the spring had to be so short!
Would that it could be prolonged like the branches of
   the willow.
Heaven seems near compared with the man who is only
   separated from me by the flowers.
How many beauties of old there have been who have
   pined away just like me!'

HUNG NIANG *says:*

   My Young Mistress is pensive and sad. I will
   make your coverlet especially fragrant. Would you
   not like to have a little sleep?

YING-YING *sings:*

   'My blue coverlet over the embroidered mattress is cold.

51

You need not make it fragrant with lily and musk
    perfumes,
Even if you used all the perfumes in the world
That would not make me feel warm and comfortable
    while I am alone.
Though it is clear that last night he was using his
    craftiness and fine poetry to lead me on,
Yet to-day I cannot get in touch with him of culture
    so great!
Of late I can neither sit nor stand steadily.
No vista now brings pleasure to me.
Even when I walk leisurely I feel wearied.
All day long, full of thoughts of love, I feel spiritless.

I will rest on my pillow, embroidered with mermaids.
When I issue from my boudoir my maid follows me
    like my shadow.
Why is it that she has become so cautious of late?
She is ever in close attendance on me,
And my mother rules me with a strict control.
The will of a maiden is easily suppressed.

You should know that whenever I see a stranger I
    become at once annoyed and displeased.
Even if he is a relation I am driven to retire by his
    disagreeable presence.
But as soon as I saw *the* man I became at once attached
    to him.
My poem the other night, in rhyme with his own,
Was as perfect in harmony as it was pure and original.
Not only were the words not forced,
Not only were the expressions natural,
But our poems were in meaning as one!

Who will act as a go-between
And go over the eastern wall to tell him of my deep love?

You are one as full of culture as of romance.
Your features indicate that you are cultivated, and your
    figure is handsome.
Undoubtedly your nature is kind, and your disposition
    is amiable.
Despite myself, I keep on repeating your name, while
    your image is imprinted on my heart.
I know that your literary talents shine as brilliantly as
    all the stars in heaven.
But who is there who will regret that your literary
    labour for ten years has remained unknown?'

> (MADAM, *entering with* FA PÊN, *knocks at the
>   door.*)

HUNG NIANG *says:*

> Why has my Mistress invited the Superior to come
> straight to our door?

> (YING-YING *sees her mother.*)

MADAM *says:*

> Have you not heard, my dear child, that Sun,
> the Flying Tiger, leading five thousand bandit
> soldiers, has surrounded the gate of the monastery?
> He says that you have black eyebrows with a
> winning expression, a face as beautiful as the lotus
> in spring, and are of such overwhelming charms as
> make you the peer of the most famous beauties of
> old. He wants to capture you forcibly and make
> you his wife and the mistress of his camp! My
> dear child, what *is* to be done?

YING-YING *sings:*

'My soul has left my body;

53

This calamity is killing me!

My tears overflow, and my sleeves cannot stop them.

There seems, at the moment, no means of escape, either
        by fleeing or remaining.

We are at a standstill, having no way to advance or to
        retire.

Where can we find a friend who will come to our rescue
        in our distress?

There is no place to which the widowed mother and
        the orphaned child can flee for protection!

Alas! at such a crisis one's thoughts first turn to my
        beloved father who is no more!

The thunder of the metal drums resounds in my ears,

The besiegers look like endless clouds,

Raising dust like torrents of rain.

It is reported that the head of the bandits says

I have black eyebrows with a winning expression,

A face as beautiful as the lotus in spring,

And I am of such overwhelming charms

As make me the peer of the most famous beauties of old.

He has a bandit host of five thousand soldiers

By which the three hundred priests

Will be, in a trice, exterminated like grass that is torn
        from its roots!

That brigand, to his family and his country, has shown
        himself a traitor.

Giving full sway to his passions, he is looting and
        robbing the people.

Not caring in the least by whom this monastery was
        erected,

He will burn it just as Chu-ko Liang set fire to the
        camp at Po-wang.'

MADAM *says:*

> Being now sixty years of age, death for me would not be premature. But you, my dear child, are still young, and are not yet married. How can this disaster, to which you have fallen victim, be allowed to overwhelm you?

YING-YING *says:*

> I think all that can be done is to hand me over to the bandit, so that the lives of all our family can be saved.

MADAM, *weeping, says:*

> Not one of the men of our family has ever committed a breach of the law, and not one of its women has married a second time. How can I bear to hand you over to the bandit? Would it not indeed be an indelible disgrace to the history of our clan?

YING-YING *says:*

> My dear mother, do not think too much about your daughter! There are five advantages in handing me over to the bandit:

She sings:

> 'Firstly, it will save my mother, the widow of the Prime Minister, from destruction;
>
> Secondly, it will prevent the monastery from being reduced to ashes;
>
> Thirdly, the priests will not suffer in any way, and will be allowed to remain in peace;
>
> Fourthly, the coffin of my late father will not be disturbed;
>
> And fifthly, my adopted brother, Huan Lang, although still young,
>
> Will be able to continue the family of the Ts'ui clan.

If I, Ying-ying, thinking only of my own safety,
Refuse to accompany the rebel host,
The monastery will be consumed in flames,
And all the priests will be spattered with blood;
The remains of my father will be reduced to dust;
Pitiable indeed will be the fate of my dear adopted
  brother,
And painful indeed will be the fate of my kind mother.

Not even a child will be left to continue our family.
If I go with the rebel host,
That will be indeed a disgrace to our family,
So the best thing for me to do is to tie a band of white
  silk around my neck
And seek death in suicide,
And present the coffin with my dead body to the
  brigand.
Thus you all will escape injury and save your lives!'

FA PÊN *says:*

> Let us all go to the preaching hall, and inquire
> from the priests and the laity, who are in the two
> corridors, if they have any good suggestions to
> offer, and we can all then go and deliberate on
> some plan that will prove effective.

> (*They all go, and arrive there.*)

MADAM *says:*

> My dear child, what is the best thing to do? I
> have something to say to you: I really cannot bear
> to be separated from you, but necessity knows no
> law. If any one among those now gathered in the
> two corridors, whether he be a priest or one of the
> laity, is able to induce the rebel host to retire, I,
> your mother, acting on my own authority, will be

56

willing to present you to him as his wife, and, contrary to the usual custom, will give him a handsome dowry. Even though such a match would be a *mésalliance*, it would be much better than falling into the hands of the brigand.

She weeps, and says:

Superior, please proclaim my proposal in loud tones in the preaching hall. My dear child, it is you who will be the sufferer!

FA PÊN *says:*

This is a better proposal!

YING-YING *sings:*

'My mother, you think of nothing but my welfare,
But consideration for me you cannot convey to others
    in a few words.
Be not anxious about my welfare.
It matters not who it may be,
So long as he can show his mettle,
By driving the rebels off with slaughter
And by repressing entirely this disturbance,
And you, contrary to the usual custom,
Are willing to give the hero a handsome dowry,
Thus effecting the union between him and me!'

FA PÊN *proclaims the above conditions, and* MR. CHANG *enters and applauds the declaration, saying:*

I have a plan for driving away the rebels. Why do you not ask me?

(*He greets* MADAM.)

FA PÊN *says:*

I beg to report to you, Madam, that this scholar is

57

my humble relative, who joined in the religious ceremony on the fifteenth of the month.

MADAM *inquires*:

What is this plan?

MR. CHANG *says*:

I beg to inform you, Madam, that handsome rewards will certainly secure brave warriors. So long as the question of reward and penalty is definitely settled my plan is sure of success.

MADAM *says*:

As I have just told the Superior: to any one who can drive off the rebels I will give my daughter as wife.

MR. CHANG *says*:

This being so, I have a plan which, first of all, requires the assistance of the Superior.

FA PÊN *says*:

An old priest such as myself is no fighter! I must ask you, sir, to find some one else to take my place.

MR. CHANG *says*:

Don't be afraid! I don't want you to fight. You go out and tell the rebel chief the important decision of Madam to the following effect: My daughter is still in mourning. If you wish to marry her, you must take off your armour, lay down your arms, and retire to the distance which an arrow could fly. You must wait for three days until the religious ceremony is finished, when she will bid farewell to her father's coffin, change into her bridal robes, and then be escorted to you. If the circumstances were different, she would be escorted to you at once. But this is impossible for

two reasons: firstly, she is still in mourning, and
secondly, it will be unlucky for your army. Go
and tell him as above.

FA PÊN *says:*

What is to happen after the three days?

MR. CHANG *says:*

I have a friend whose surname is Tu, his name
Ch'üeh, who is entitled the General of the White
Horse, and is now in command of an army of a
hundred thousand men which is guarding the P'u
Pass. He and I are sworn brothers and most
intimate. If I write a letter to him he is sure to
come to my rescue.

FA PÊN *says:*

Madam, if the General of the White Horse actually
does come there is no need to be afraid even if
there were a hundred Flying Tigers! Please set
your mind at rest, Madam!

MADAM *says:*

This being so, our warmest thanks are due to this
gentleman. Hung Niang, see your Young Mistress
back to her chamber.

YING-YING *says:*

Hung Niang, we are indeed much indebted to him!

She sings:

'All the priests and the attendants have fled for their lives,
But for our family who has any care?
Though he is not acquainted with us and is a mere
    outsider, he is anxious for us.
It is not a case of a scholar who wishes to show his
    wisdom by giving advice,

59

But he desires to save his own life, so that what is
    ordinary and extraordinary should not perish
    together!
What near relation have I to take pity on my fate, which
    hangs on a thread?
Success or failure depends entirely on this scholar!
His tactical writing is worthy of the famous generals of
    old, who were able to secure order at home and
    conquer the enemy abroad.
Merely with the point of his pen, he is able to sweep
    away five thousand men!'

[*Exeunt* YING-YING *and* HUNG NIANG.

FA PÊN, *in a loud voice, says:*
    I request the General to come for a conference.

The FLYING TIGER *enters with soldiers, and says:*
    Send Ying-ying to me at once!

FA PÊN *says:*
    Calm your wrath, General! Madam Ts'ui has
    issued her orders, which I am to convey to you.
    (*He repeats the order.*)

The FLYING TIGER *says:*
    That being so, I limit you to three days. If Ying-
    ying is not sent to me within that time I will have
    you, one and all, put to death. You tell Madam
    what an excellent son-in-law I will make! And
    say she ought to accept me.

[*Exit the* FLYING TIGER *with the soldiers.*

FA PÊN *says:*
    The bandits have retired. You must write your
    letter without delay, sir.

MR. CHANG *says:*

> I have already written the letter, which I have here, and all that is necessary is to have it sent.

FA PÊN *says:*

> I have a disciple in the kitchen called Hui-ming whose strong points are drinking and fighting. If you simply ask him to act as messenger he is sure to refuse; but if you can arouse his perverse spirit nothing will deter him from going. He is really the only man upon whom we can rely.

MR. CHANG, *in a loud voice, says:*

> I have a letter to send to the General of the White Horse. I cannot allow Hui-ming of the kitchen to take it. Who among the others of the community will dare to take it?

HUI-MING *enters and says:*

> I insist upon going with it. I say I insist!

He sings:

> 'I recite not "The Lotus of the Good Law",
> And I have no respect for the "*Liang Huang Ch'an*"!
> I have thrown away my monk's cowl,
> And I have doffed my one-sleeve robe;
> My desire for slaughter stimulates my heroic courage,
> And now I arm myself with the iron poker which resembles the tail of the black dragon!
>
> It is not a question of my being ambitious, or being forward;
> How can I know anything about what they called worshipping Buddha?
> What I do understand is how, with bold strides, to enter the Tiger's den and the Dragon's pool and there deal a slaughter!

It is not a question of my being greedy, or being bold;
But the diet of vegetables and bread which I have had
  to eat is truly tasteless.
If I can devour those five thousand men raw, without
  having them roasted, baked, fried, or stewed,
The blood of their throats will for a time quench my
  thirst.
The heart within their entrails will at once satisfy my
  greedy appetite.
What is there of them that would be repugnant to my
  taste?

Your thin soups, thick noodles, mixed flour dumplings,
  pickled yellow leeks, strong-smelling bean-curd are
  quite tasteless.
With ten thousand catties of flour, though of poor
  quality,
I will make dumplings with those five thousand men
  as minced meat.
Deter me not, deter me not!
And if any of their flesh is left over
I will sprinkle it with salt to have it preserved!'

FA PÊN *says:*

Hui-ming, Mr. Chang, the graduate, does not
wish to employ you, but still you insist on going;
are you really daring enough to go or not?

HUI-MING *sings:*

'Ask me not whether I dare to go or not;
But I want to ask you, my Superior: Do you really wish
  to employ me or not?
You say that the fame of this Flying Tiger is equal to
  that of a real tiger,

But that fellow is only a creature of lust and greed;
How can he be endured for a moment?'

MR. CHANG *says:*

> How is it that you, who have left your family to
> become a monk, do not recite your sacred books
> and study your magical charms, and accompany
> your teachers for spiritual instruction to their
> lecture halls, but want to act as bearer of my letter?

HUI-MING *sings:*

'Our sacred books I shrink from discussing;
Religious meditation I have no time to enter into;
My knife I have newly polished,
And it is without a trace of tarnish!
All the others of the community, who are neither
    women nor men,
In broad daylight, lazily shut the doors of their cells;
What care they whether the precious monastery is on
    fire or not!
To the man who is skilled in literature and an expert
    in military affairs, and who is a thousand miles
    from here,
If you want to send this letter which will bring relief
    from your difficulties and support you in your peril,
I am the man with the courage who will not disgrace
    the commission!'

MR. CHANG *says:*

> Will you go by yourself, or do you require some-
> body to assist you?

HUI-MING *sings:*

'Arrange to send with me several young monks carrying
    banners and parasols;

And some weakling acolytes with rolling-pins and
   pokers,
While you are maintaining a firm attitude, so as to
   pacify the whole community of monks,
And I will boldly go forward to meet the force of
   bandits.'

MR. CHANG *says:*

   Supposing they stop you! What will you do?

HUI-MING *says:*

   How can they dare to stop me? You may make
   your mind easy on that score.

He sings:

   'One angry glance of mine is sufficient to make the calm
      sea rough;
   One roar of my voice will make the hills and cliffs
      re-echo;
   One step of mine will create an earthquake;
   By raising my arm I will make Heaven's gates shake!

   Those afar, in one swipe, I will wipe out with my iron
      poker;
   Those near, with ready ease I will cut in two with my
      knife;
   My enemies, small in dimension, I will pick up and
      treat as a football;
   Those who are larger I will seize and smash their skulls
      into pieces!'

MR. CHANG *says:*

   If I give you the letter now, when will you be able
   to start?

HUI-MING *sings:*

   'I have always been of a nature bold and intrepid,

64

And I know not what fear means;
I am never weary of fighting,
Heaven having made me a mass of bravery;
In all matters, easy or difficult, I have invariably acted
    with determination,
Unlike those who fiddle about, unable to come to a
    decision;
Even to meet death will cause me no regret.
With knife and sword in hand, I am not one who will
    stay his onward rush against the foe!

I have always been one who am ready to overcome the
    strong and to yield to the weak,
And have always preferred the bitter to the sweet.
You must not send me on a fool's errand on account of
    your matrimonial intentions.
If General Tu will not disperse the armed rebels for
    you,
Then the responsibility of your love-affair will depend
    entirely on yourself.
Though you may speak fair words,
A mistake once made
Will cause you shame for the rest of your life.'

He says:
        I am off!

He sings:
    'You sound the drum three times to help to stimulate
        my spirits,
    While I, with the blessing of Buddha, utter a loud
        war-cry.
    When the embroidered banners are displayed, you will
        see afar a hero in me.

65

Behold, the courage of the five thousand bandits, at the
first threat, oozes!'

MR. CHANG *says:*

Madam, you may tell the Young Lady to be easy
in her mind. As soon as the letter arrives the
martial force will come at once.

'The letter, which flies by night,

Will bring the White Horse General as if from Heaven!'

[*Exeunt.*

GENERAL TU *enters with his soldiers, and says:*

My surname is Tu, and my name is Ch'üeh, and
my style is Chün-shih. My native place is to the
east of Lo-yang. In my youth I studied the Confucian classics with Chang Chün-jui. Afterwards
I gave up literary for military studies, and came
out first on the list of military graduates. I was
appointed *Generalissimo* of the Western Punitive
Expedition, and now I am Field-Marshal in command of a hundred thousand men to guard the
P'u Pass. A man has arrived from the Ho-chung
Prefecture, from whom I learned that my sworn
brother, Chün-jui, is at present staying in P'u
Chiu Monastery. I cannot understand why he
does not come to see me. Recently, Ting Wên-ya
has been discharging his duties in an irregular
manner, and allowing his troops to plunder the
population. I must get ready a force and wipe
them all out before I have my breakfast. But I do
not know exactly the true facts of the case; I dare
not act without due consideration. Yesterday I
dispatched some intelligence officers to make
inquiries. Now I am going to my tent to see
whether they have come with any information
regarding the army to report.

(*He opens the entrance of his tent and sits down.*)

66

HUI-MING *enters, and says:*

Having left the P'u Chiu Monastery, I have lost no time in reaching the P'u Pass. Here is the encampment of General Tu. I must go in at once.

(*He is arrested by some soldiers, who report to the* GENERAL.)

TU *says:*

Hallo, monk! Whose spy are you?

HUI-MING *says:*

I am not a spy. I am a monk of the P'u Chiu Monastery, where at present the Flying Tiger, Sun, is creating a terrible disturbance. He has surrounded the monastery with five thousand bandit soldiers and wishes to carry off by force the daughter of the former Prime Minister, Ts'ui, and make her his wife. A visitor named Chang Chün-jui has written a letter to you, and has sent me with it in the hope that Your Excellency will at once relieve them from their perilous situation.

TU *says:*

Attendants, release the monk. Chang Chün-jui is my sworn brother. Hand his letter to me at once.

HUI-MING *prostrates himself and delivers the letter, which* TU *opens and reads:*

'Your former fellow-student and younger brother, Chang Kung, makes his bow, once, and again, and presents this letter to Your Excellency, Chün Shih, his beloved elder brother, the great *Generalissimo*. Two years have passed since I was last in your noble presence. At night, when the wind blows and the rain falls, you are always in my thoughts. When I left my home to go to the Capital, I passed Ho-chung on the way, and intended to visit you so as to have a chat about what has happened since we last met. But the journey had so exhausted me that I suddenly became ill. I am now somewhat better, and there is no cause for anxiety. As I am travelling with light baggage, I am taking a short rest in a quiet monastery. Suddenly my quarters became a scene of arms. Since the death of the former Minister, Ts'ui, many troubles have arisen in his family. His widow has brought his coffin to the monastery so that it may rest there temporarily pending the holding of the usual religious ceremony. But, quite unexpectedly, an outrageous intruder, at the sight of the beautiful daughter, has collected a host numbering five thousand and is about to act in the most outrageous manner. Who has no young, defenceless children? The moment I saw their helpless state I was overwhelmed with fury and felt that only the extermination of the bandits would give me satisfaction. But, to my regret, during my whole life I have never been able even to truss a chicken. Even if I sacrifice my unimportant life, it would be far from having the least effect. But then I reflected that you, my beloved elder brother, have received full powers to control a specified locality, and are able to rule a storm of wind and clouds with a word of command. You, my beloved elder brother, carrying on the tradition of the heroes of old, are in no way unworthy of the famous Shao-hu. I am now in great danger; the matter is most pressing and seems hopeless. Words fail to express my longing for your help. I beseech and pray you to come, with your banners waving, to Ho-chung, as quickly as lightning; starting in the morning, you will arrive in the evening. So that we, the fish stranded on dry land, will have no reason to hate the Great

West River for refusing help. And the late
Minister, Ts'ui, in the Shades below, will also be
eternally grateful. Hoping you will give this
matter attention, Chang Kung again salutes you.
Written on the sixteenth day of the second moon.'

TU *says:*

'This being so, I will at once issue orders. Monk,
you go back ahead, and I will follow this very
night. By the time you have reached the monastery, probably I shall have captured the brigand
already.

HUI-MING *says:*

Affairs in the monastery are in a very critical
condition. Your Excellency must go as quickly as
possible.   [*Exit.*

TU *issues orders, and says:*

Officers and soldiers of the three armies, listen to
my orders. Select five thousand most reliable
soldiers of the infantry and cavalry and let them
depart this very night; and go directly to the P'u
Chiu Monastery in the Ho-chung Prefecture, in
order to relieve my younger brother.

ALL *answer:*

Your orders will be obeyed.   [*Exeunt.*

SUN *rushes in with soldiers and says:*

The General of the White Horse has come. What
is to be done? What is to be done? We must all
dismount, doff our armour, throw down our spears,
and kneel down. Everything depends on what the
General decides to do with us.

TU *enters with soldiers:*

Why have you all dismounted, doffed your armour,

69

thrown down your spears, and knelt down? Do you expect me to forgive you? All right! I will order that only Sun, the Flying Tiger, is to be beheaded. As for the rest, those who do not want to continue to be soldiers may all return to their farming; those who wish to continue may give a list of their names and I will enlist them.

[*Exeunt all the bandits.*

MADAM, *with* FA PÊN, *enters, and says:*

The letter was sent two days ago, but I have seen no reply.

MR. CHANG *enters, and says:*

Outside the monastery gate the sound of obeying orders is as loud as thunder; probably my elder brother has arrived.

(TU *and* CHANG *meet and bow to one another.*)

MR. CHANG *says:*

Since I last left your honourable presence I have for so long been deprived of your instructions that our personal meeting to-day seems like a dream.

TU *says:*

I have just heard that you were travelling in my neighbourhood. I have not been able to visit you, for which omission I beg that you will forgive me.

(TU *and* MADAM *meet and bow to one another.*)

MADAM *says:*

My widowed self and my orphaned daughter have reached such an extreme crisis that death seemed inevitable. But, thanks to you, you have to-day given us new life.

70

TU *says:*

> I have failed to take proper precautions against the outrageous acts of these vile bandits, with the result that you have been alarmed; for which failure I deserve to die ten thousand deaths.

To MR. CHANG:

> May I ask you, my worthy younger brother, why you did not come to my place?

MR. CHANG *says:*

> I happened to be slightly indisposed, that is the reason why I failed to visit you. To-day I ought to accompany you on your return, but Madam yesterday promised to give me her beloved daughter in marriage, and I wonder if I may venture to trouble you to act as go-between. My idea is that a month after the great ceremony has been completed I should visit you and offer my humble thanks.

TU *says:*

> My hearty congratulations and best wishes to you, madam. Of course I will act as go-between.

MADAM *says:*

> There are other arrangements which I have in mind. In the meantime let tea and dinner be got ready.

TU *says:*

> As five thousand men have just surrendered, I must go and deal with the matter. I will certainly come some other time to renew my congratulations.

MR. CHANG *says:*

> I dare not detain my brother lest it might interfere with his military duties.

> > (TU *mounts his horse.*)

71

'The Mounted Horseman leaves the P'u Chiu Monastery amid clashing of brazen cymbals,
While his soldiers, following him to the P'u Pass, raise
shouts of victory.'   [*Exit* GENERAL TU.

MADAM *says:*

> Mr. Chang, we can never forget your great kind-
ness. From now onwards you must give up your
present quarters in the monastery and move to the
library of our quarters and make yourself comfortable there. I will to-morrow prepare a light
repast and will order our maid, Hung Niang, to go
to invite your presence. You must make a point
of coming.   [*Exit.*

MR. CHANG *bids good-bye to* FA PÊN, *and says:*

> I am going to pack up my things and remove to
the library.

'The fiery beacons of war, rashly ignited by the bold
bandits,
Have happily resulted in bringing a fair lady to her
wooer!'

> Flying Tiger, Sun, I am eternally grateful to you.

FA PÊN *says:*

> Mr. Chang, when you have leisure you must come
as formerly to my room and have a chat.
>   [*Exeunt.*

ACT II

THE INVITATION TO THE FEAST

MR. CHANG *enters and says:*

> Yesterday evening Madam said that she was going to send me an invitation to a feast by Hung Niang. I rose before daylight to await her arrival, but up to the present I have seen nothing of her. Oh! where is the precious Hung Niang?

HUNG NIANG *enters, and says:*

> My Mistress has ordered me to invite Mr. Chang. So I must go as quickly as possible.

She sings:

> 'Five thousand bandit soldiers,
> Like the floating clouds
> Have been in a moment wiped out,
> And our whole family, in the midst of death, has found
>   life again.
> With minds relieved, we should return thanks to the
>   gods,
> Worshipping them with due religious ceremonies;
> And to Chang Chün-jui we must manifest our admira-
>   tion and respect.
> The hopes that seemed formerly vain
> Have been fulfilled by the intervention of a letter.
>
> To-day the Eastern Pavilion, wreathed in mist, is
>   opened for you,

73

And no longer need you wait in the Western Chamber
with the moon overhead.
The thin coverlet and the lonely pillow, there will now
be some one to make warm,
And henceforward you will never feel cold.
To you a great joy will be the sweet-scented fragrance
arising from the precious incense-burner,
The gentle breeze wafted through the embroidered
curtains,
And the tranquillity that reigns within the green
windows.'

She says:
I have already arrived at the library.

She sings:
'In this quiet and secluded spot
Can there be any wayfarer?
Here the green moss
Is dotted with the glistening dew.
Outside the window I must cough once.'

MR. CHANG *says:*
Who is it?

HUNG NIANG *says:*
It is I.

(MR. CHANG, *opening the door, sees her.*)

HUNG NIANG *sings:*
'Opening the red door, he makes all haste to inquire,

Greeting me with hands clasped and such incessant
ceremonial bows
That I am unable to respond with my own salutations.

He presents a brilliant appearance, wearing a hat of
    black gauze,
And being attired in a graduate's robe of pure white,
With a belt exposing a brilliantly gilded buckle,

With his splendid garments as an added attraction to
    his fine presence,
How could he fail to touch the heart of Ying-ying!
By his looks, his talents, and his nature
He has moved me to admiration, hard-hearted though
    I always have been.

She says:

    I am here, by Madam's orders. . . .

MR. CHANG *says:*

    I am off at once!

HUNG NIANG *sings:*

'Before I could say a word he kept on answering me
    repeatedly and hastily,
As if he wished to fly to Ying-ying,
Saying without ceasing, "My Lady, I come, I come!"
Graduates, when they receive an invitation,
Regard it as if it were a military order,
Which their empty stomachs make them only too eager
    to obey.'

MR. CHANG *says:*

    May I venture to ask you, Miss Hung Niang, why
    this banquet is being held? Will there be other
    guests present?

HUNG NIANG *sings:*

'In the first place, it is in order to allay alarm,
And secondly, to thank you for what you have done.

She has not invited any neighbours or relations to be
    present;
And she does not wish to receive any gifts.
Keeping away all the priests,
She invites Your Honour
In order to betroth Ying-ying to you.
I see that he is only too ready to obey the summons
    to the feast,

But that, as he struts to and fro, he looks admiringly at
    his own shadow.
The crazy Graduate, the poor mad Scholar,
Has taken such pains to polish his head,
That flies might slither on it,
And its brilliance might dazzle one's eyes.
He looks such a poor, miserable wretch that he sets
    one's teeth on edge.
He has to arrange to seal and lock up a scanty portion
    of decayed rice
And carefully cover a few jars of pickled turnips.

But this man, having shown himself so clever in one
    matter, is sure to be clever in everything,
Thus differing completely from him who, failing in one
    thing, fails in everything.
In this world plants and trees, although said to be
    without sentiments,
Still grow in unison;
How can a young man like this be free from love-
    sickness?
Heaven has endowed him with such lofty intelligence,
And such pure taste in the matter of dress.
Night after night he has to spend in solitude.

I have always heard that a man of genius is prone to
 be full of love,
And that if he meets a beauty who treats him slight-
 ingly
This may often result in his renouncing existence.
Of the good faith and the true sincerity of my Young
 Mistress
To-night you will have good proof.

But of a joy and happiness such as will happen
 to-night
The gentle and delicate Ying-ying has never had any
 experience.
You must be calm and kind.
When in the light of the lamp you are joined in happy
 unison,
And after you have seen all her bewitching and killing
 beauty,
You will not be able to restrain your ardour.'

MR. CHANG *says*:

May I venture to ask Miss Hung Niang what
decorations have been arranged there for to-day?
How can I possibly go there without having made
due preparation?

HUNG NIANG *sings*:

'The ground there is covered with flowers, red as rouge.
Don't miss the happy hour and the gay scene.
My Mistress has ordered me not to delay;
I request you, sir, not to fail to go at once.
We have prepared a bridal chamber in which hangs a
 curtain sprinkled with gold and embroidered with
 a midnight moon and the birds of love;

77

And a screen of soft and warm jade, ornamented with
    peacocks enjoying the breezes of spring.
While melody of happy harmony will be played,
Accompanied by the male phoenix flute, the ivory
    castanets,
The wild swan lute, and the female phoenix organ.'

MR. CHANG *says:*

> May I venture to ask you, Miss Hung Niang,
> as I am a traveller, and have nothing whatever
> that I can present as a ceremonial gift, how can I
> possibly go to see Madam?

HUNG NIANG *sings:*

'When no betrothal money is necessary,
The marriage can be celebrated at once.
This happy union has been determined by Heaven.
To-day you both are fated to ride—one the male and
    the other the female phoenix,
And to-night I will be able to see the Cow-herd and the
    Spinning-maiden enjoying each other's company.
You are indeed very fortunate.
Without having necessitated the tying of even a shred
    of the red silk,
You are henceforward joined together for life!

Methinks your merit in having extinguished the
    rebels,
And having been able to enlist the aid of the General,
Has been quite as effective as if the red thread had
    fixed the union.
The heart of Ying-ying you have already entirely won.
For in your breast there are a million soldiers.
From of old literary talent has held first place;
When have you ever seen a man who enjoys the

company of a fair maiden, adorned with pearls
and jade,
And who comes not from among the groups of students
who study old books by a dim light?
My Mistress here has only her own family,
And you, sir, have no companions:
Free from all fuss,
It will indeed be a quiet ceremony;
They invite only you, their loyal benefactor, the man
of their heart;
And they are avoiding the monks in the monastery, who
heed not worldly matters.
The command of my Mistress must not be disobeyed,
therefore pray accompany me at once.'

MR. CHANG *says:*

Such being the case, you, Miss Hung Niang, go
first, and I will follow directly.

HUNG NIANG *sings:*

'You must not be too modest, sir,
My Mistress awaits you, and you only.
From of old, to obey is better than to be merely polite.
Do not compel me to come a second time to invite you.'

MR. CHANG *says:*   [*Exit.*

Hung Niang has departed, so I now close the door
of the library. When I arrive in the presence of
Madam she will say: 'So you have come, Mr.
Chang. You and my Ying-ying, forming a happy
couple, must drink two cups of wine before you
depart for the bridal chamber to become man and
wife.' (*He laughs.*) Flying Tiger, Sun, you are
indeed my great benefactor! I owe much to him.
Some other day, when I have leisure, I will make

a point of spending ten thousand cash of good money, and ask Fa Pên to perform a religious ceremony to save the soul of Flying Tiger.

'My sincere hope is that the heavenly dragon will send
 down the rain of the Law,
So as secretly to help the Flying Tiger to ascend on the
 morning clouds to Paradise.'   [*Exit*.

ACT III

THE BREACH OF PROMISE

MADAM *enters, and says:*

> Hung Niang has gone to invite Mr. Chang. Why has she not yet returned?

HUNG NIANG *enters, and, seeing* MADAM, *says:*

> Mr. Chang told me to go on ahead and he will follow later.

> (MR. CHANG *enters, and salutes* MADAM.)

MADAM *says:*

> If it had not been for you the other day, Mr. Chang, how could we have survived till to-day! The fact that all my family is still alive is entirely due to you. I have prepared just a small feast. Though it is not in any way a return for what you have done for us, I hope you will not regard it as entirely unworthy.

MR. CHANG *says:*

> On the good fortune of one person everybody else depends. The defeat of this bandit was entirely due to the good fortune of Madam. This is a thing of the past and is not worthy of mention.

MADAM *says:*

> Bring the wine here. You, sir, drink off this cup.

MR. CHANG *says:*

How could I presume to refuse that which my elder bestows on me!

(*He at once drinks and pours out wine for* MADAM.)

MADAM *says:*

Please sit down, sir.

MR. CHANG *says:*

It is my duty to remain standing by your side. How could I dare to sit down in your presence!

MADAM *says:*

Don't you know the old saying: Politeness is not so good as obedience?

(MR. CHANG, *asking to be excused, sits down.*)

(MADAM *tells* HUNG NIANG *to ask her* YOUNG MISTRESS *to come.*)

YING-YING *enters, and says:*

'Now that our enemies, like mist and wind, have been rapidly dispersed and peace has been restored to the land,

Both the Sun and the Moon will illumine our splendid feast.'

She sings:

'Had it not been that the graduate Chang had such a wide acquaintance

How could any other person have made the armed bandits retreat?

The banquet is spread,

And arrangements have been made for music and song.

The delicate, twirling smoke of the incense

　　And the subdued fragrance of the flowers
　　Are wafted by the east wind around the curtains.
　　To him who has rescued all of us from disaster
　　It is but just and proper to show special attention,
　　And right and fitting to treat him with every respect.'

HUNG NIANG *says:*

　　My Young Mistress, you have got up very early
　　this morning.

YING-YING *sings:*

　　'I have just painted my eyebrows near the window
　　　curtained with green gauze,
　　And wiped away the fragrant powder which was soiling
　　　my silk robes,
　　And with the tip of my fingers I have gently adjusted
　　　my hair-pin.
　　If I had not been disturbed and awakened,
　　I would still be asleep under my embroidered coverlet.'

HUNG NIANG *says:*

　　My Young Mistress, you have finished your toilet
　　very early. Have you washed your hands? Your
　　complexion appears to me to be so delicate that
　　even to breathe on it or touch it would hurt it.
　　What a lucky man you are, Mr. Chang!

YING-YING *sings:*

　　'Don't you see that you are jabbering there and talking
　　　nonsense, without rhyme or reason,
　　When you say that my complexion is so beautiful that
　　　even to breathe on it or touch it would hurt it?'

HUNG NIANG *says:*

　　My Young Mistress was truly created by Heaven
　　to be the wife of a nobleman!

YING-YING *sings:*

'You must stop your noisy babble.
One should not talk glibly at random.
How do you know whether he is fortunate or not?
And whether I, as the wife of a nobleman, will pass
     muster?'

HUNG NIANG *says:*

Formerly both of you used to be sad, but to-day
you are very happy.

YING-YING *sings:*

'All you can say is that my love-sickness is on his
     account, his love-sickness is on my account,
And that from to-day our love-sickness will be cured!
This is an occasion on which our gratitude should be
     shown by a special feast.
Mother, you worry too much about money!'

HUNG NIANG *says:*

When my Young Mistress is to marry Mr. Chang,
why is a big banquet not spread and relatives and
friends not invited? Why is it that only a small
feast is prepared?

YING-YING *says:*

You don't know my mother's mind!

She sings:

'Being afraid that I shall cause loss to the family on
     account of my dowry,
She is showing our gratitude and celebrating my mar-
     riage by one feast instead of two!
His having invoked the aid of the General to exterminate
     the bandits

84

Is worthy of all the money our family can give him for
 the rest of his life.
What have you spent to effect this union of us both?
You must not show yourself a stingy mother by always
 considering money
And fearing to spend too much!

Outside the curtain of the door,
Before my small feet enter,
I take a furtive glance with my eyes, which resemble
 the autumn waves.'

MR. CHANG *says:*

 Please excuse me for a moment.

  (*He pretends to have met* YING-YING *by
  accident.*)

YING-YING *sings:*

 'Who would have thought that he would show himself
  possessed of such insight as to see through me at
  once!
 This has so startled me as to make me retreat.'

MADAM *says:*

 Come nearer, my daughter, and pay your respects
 to your elder brother.

MR. CHANG *says:*

 Ah, those words are not of good augury!

YING-YING *says:*

 Oh, my mother has changed her mind!

HUNG NIANG *says:*

 Oh, their love-sickness has received its death-blow!

YING-YING *sings:*

'I see him as if in the midst of thorns, unable to move,
As if he had fainted and had not come to life again.
In utter confusion he is unable to reply;
Lifeless and dispirited, he cannot crouch or sit!

'You are indeed a nice old lady!
Why should I, your daughter, call him my elder
    brother?
I am suddenly separated from my lover, who may be
    compared with him who was overwhelmed in the
    white waves while keeping his tryst at the Blue
    Bridge,
Or with him who, missing his beloved, in fury set fire
    to the Temple of the Fire God, which was con-
    sumed in flames,
Or like the two ever-inseparable fish with one eye
    apiece are forced apart by the pure, green sea
    waves.
Why should I feel so worried and agitated?
Why should my eyebrows be knit in sorrow?

With lowered head, showing my white neck,
With my black locks all undone,
And much perplexed in mind,
What possible chance is there for me to hold converse
    with him when we do meet?
My eyes that were once brilliant as stars have now lost
    their sparkle,
My fragrant breath is now consumed in sighs,
My sorrow seems too great to bear.
This feast is truly like a gathering of crows which soon
    disperses.'

MADAM *says:*

> Hung Niang, bring some heated wine so that your Young Mistress may fill a cup for her elder brother.

> (YING-YING *fills a cup for him.*)

MR. CHANG *says:*

> I am not a drinker.

YING-YING *says:*

> Hung Niang, remove the wine-cup.

YING-YING *sings:*

'He is really unable to drink even nectar.
Who could have believed that the happiness to be en-
    joyed in the Western Chamber in the moonlight
Would become an empty dream!
Tears imperceptibly fill his eyes,
And, as if beside himself, he wipes them away, soaking
    the sleeve of his silk robe.
Listlessly he tries to open his eyes,
And spiritless he becomes an immovable lump!
He cannot lift his hands, nor even shrug his shoulders.
He appears to be so incurably ill
That it seems impossible that he can continue to live.
Mother, you have driven him to death.
What more is there to be said?'

MADAM *says:*

> My daughter, you absolutely must fill a cup of wine for your elder brother.

> (YING-YING *fills a cup of wine.*)

MR. CHANG *says:*

> I have already said that I am not a drinker.

'YOU WILL FIND THAT WHEN THE WINE MOUNTS,

'YOUR HEART WILL BE MORE AT EASE'

Y‌ING-YING *says:*

Mr. Chang, please receive the cup of wine.

She sings:

'A miserable cup of wine I present to you,
Who bend your head in silence as if you no longer wish
  to exist.
You do not look very intoxicated.
Do you refuse because the glass cup is too large?
If you will follow my advice, you will find that when the
  wine mounts, your heart will be more at ease.

Now your trouble and sorrow may be bearable,
But as time goes on and your thoughts dwell on them,
  what is to be done then?
I should now like to tell you what the feelings of my
  heart are;
But how can I do so since my mother is seated at my
  side?
And though I am separated from you
By only a short distance, you seem to be as far off as
  Heaven!'

(M‌R. C‌HANG *drinks the cup of wine.*)

(Y‌ING-YING *sits down at the feast.*)

M‌ADAM *says:*

Hung Niang, pour out some more wine. You, sir,
must drink this cup empty.

(M‌R. C‌HANG *does not respond.*)

Y‌ING-YING *sings:*

'Although you have devised a means of getting out of
  your difficulty,
Others have for long guessed what you thought a riddle.

While you still, with your honeyed words, try to
    console people,
You only make them still more unhappy!

The fate of beauties is ever wretched;
And the scholar is ever a coward!
Sad is the orphan without a father's guidance,
And abandoned is the daughter whose marriage may
    cost so much.
I know not what my mother will do with me!'

(MR. CHANG *smiles ironically.*)

YING-YING *sings:*

'You think that he is inclined to laugh loudly?
In his heart of hearts he is filled with tears!
Had it not been for the letter which led to the defeat
    of the rebels
How could any one of our family have survived!
If it is not his desire to marry me, what then is his
    desire?
It is impossible even to guess.
Your powers of deception are as extensive as the
    heavens,
Success or failure in this matter entirely rests with you,
    mother!

From now henceforward my powdered face will remain
    as pale as the blossoms of the pear,
And my lips will no longer be as red as the cherry.
When will my love-sickness receive its cure?
My sorrow is as profound as the black sea,
As extensive as the earth,
And as immense as the azure sky!

You first looked up to him as if he could help you like
the spirit of T'ai Hêng Mountain,
And that you hungered and thirsted for his relief as if
he were the god of the Eastern Ocean.
But how bitterly cruel you are to him!
You are crumpling the tender twin buds of the flower,
Severing the fragrant lovers' knot,
And destroying the two beautiful branches joined
together in union.
It is well known that the burdens of old age should be
relieved;
But who would have thought that the hopes of youth
would be disappointed?
You have shattered our future which betokened such
brilliance;
On the one hand you have vainly flattered him with
sugary words,
On the other you have tried to trick me by falsely
calling me his sister!'

MADAM *says*:

Hung Niang, conduct your Young Mistress to her
bed-chamber.

(YING-YING *bids good-bye to* MR. CHANG.)

[*Exeunt* YING-YING *and* HUNG NIANG.

MR. CHANG *says*:

I am overcome with wine and beg to bid Madam
farewell. If I may be permitted, I should like
to express my feelings. Formerly, when the outrageous bandits wished to give vent to their
violence, and calamity seemed likely to occur at any
moment, Madam said: 'To him who can make the

bandits withdraw I will give Ying-ying as wife.'
Were not those your actual words?

MADAM *says:*

They were.

MR. CHANG *says:*

At that time, who was it who came forward boldly
to the rescue?

MADAM *says:*

To you, sir, we certainly do owe our lives. But
when the late Prime Minister was alive——

MR. CHANG *says:*

Please stop a moment, Madam. At that time I
wrote the letter in all haste, requesting General Tu
to come. Was that only because I wanted something to eat and drink to-day? When this morning
Hung Niang, under your orders, came to summon
me, I thought that you were going to fulfil your
promise and that I was about to have the happiness
of marrying your beautiful daughter. I do not
know what has made you suddenly fling at us the
titles of elder brother and younger sister. Allow
me to ask you what possible use can the Young
Lady have for me as an elder brother and what use
can I have for her as a younger sister? As the
proverb says: 'It is never too late to mend.' I
request you, Madam, to reconsider the matter
carefully.

MADAM *says:*

As regards my daughter, when the late Prime
Minister was alive he had actually betrothed her
to my nephew Chêng Hêng, and I have already
written to summon him. If he comes, what am I
to do? I now wish to reward you with a large sum

of money, and hope that you will select some other lady of an influential and noble family, so that both of us may carry out our matrimonial arrangements to our mutual satisfaction. This would seem to be advantageous for us both.

MR. CHANG *says:*

Do you really think so? But supposing General Tu had not come and the Flying Tiger, Sun, had carried out his outrageous intention without restraint, what would you have had to say then? What use have I for your money? I will now bid you farewell without further ado!

MADAM *says:*

Stay a moment, sir! You have been drinking to-day! Hung Niang, support the elder brother to the library to rest there. To-morrow we will discuss other arrangements.   [*Exit.*

HUNG NIANG *enters, and, supporting* MR. CHANG, *says:*

Mr. Chang, would it not have been better if you had drunk a cup less?

MR. CHANG *says:*

Alas! Miss Hung Niang, you are very simple. What wine have I drunk? Since I saw the Young Lady I have had neither food nor sleep, and up to the present moment have endured no end of sufferings. I cannot tell this to others, but it is useless to attempt to deceive you. Regarding the matter of the other day, the letter I wrote is certainly not worthy of mention; but Madam, who is a lady of the First Rank, and whose utterance is as good as gold and whose words are as precious as jade, made an agreement with me, promising me her daughter in marriage. Miss Hung Niang, her promise was not only heard by us two, but by innumerable priests and members of the laity in both corridors; and, furthermore, also by the Buddha and Heaven above, and by the Protectors of the Law below! But now, unexpectedly, she has suddenly changed her plans and reduced me to my wits' end without being able to find any way out of the difficulty. When will this matter end? It seems that all I can do is to unloose my girdle and commit suicide (by hanging myself with it) before your eyes.

'Pitiable, indeed, is the traveller who hangs on the beam within the closed doors,

And who actually becomes a ghost far away from his native home and village.' (*He unlooses his girdle.*)

HUNG NIANG *says:*

Don't be so rash! I understand thoroughly your sentiments for my Young Mistress. As to the incident of the other day, it was really owing to my having been entirely unacquainted with you, and the whole matter was so sudden that you should not blame me if I have offended you in any way. As regards the present matter, there is no doubt that Madam did make a promise to you. Besides, as Confucius said: 'One good deed deserves another', and I must do my best to help.

MR. CHANG *says:*

If you do I shall be for ever grateful. But what means will you adopt to carry out your plans?

HUNG NIANG *says:*

I have seen that you in a case have a lute, on which you must be an expert player. My Young Mistress is passionately devoted to the music of the lute. To-night my Young Mistress and I must go without fail to the garden to burn incense. I will cough as a signal, and when you hear it you should begin to play. I will observe carefully what my Young Mistress says, and at the right moment I will tell her the sentiments of your heart. If she says anything, I will report it to you the first thing to-morrow morning. My Mistress may at any moment be calling me, so I had better go back at once.   [*Exit.*

R. CHANG *says*:

'As formerly, I have to spend the night alone in the solitary monastery,

With no hope to-night of the joys of her bridal chamber.'
                                                  [*Exit.*

ACT IV

LOVE AND THE LUTE

MR. CHANG *enters, and says:*

Miss Hung Niang told me to wait in the garden to-night, while her Young Mistress is burning incense, and to play on the lute a tune expressing the sentiments of my heart in order to test her feelings and see what she will say. Careful reflection on this suggestion shows it to be most reasonable. The night is dark. Oh, Moon, can you not, for my sake, come out a little earlier! Oh, I have just heard the beat of the drum! Oh, I have just heard the ringing of the bell!

He tunes his lute, and says:

Oh, my Lute, my companion by lake and sea! on you I entirely depend for the great success of this matter. Oh, Heaven, will you not, for my sake, lend a gentle breeze to waft the sound of my lute to the ears of my Young Lady, ears as if carved from jade and as if moulded of white powder, which can appreciate the music and are beautiful to behold!

> (YING-YING, *accompanied by* HUNG NIANG, *enters.*)

HUNG NIANG *says:*

My Young Mistress, let us go to burn incense. How very bright the moon is!

YING-YING *says:*

Hung Niang, how can I have the heart to go to

burn incense? Oh, Moon, why have you come forth?

She sings:

'The moon has suddenly come forth in a cloudless sky;

The wind-swept blossoms of the red flowers are scattered on the steps, making them fragrant;

My separation has filled me with endless regrets, and my indescribable sorrows are without number!

Oh, my mother, it seldom happens that a good beginning makes a good end.

He has been to me a lover as unreal as a mirage,

While I have been to him as a mere picture of one beloved!

I am only allowed to cherish him in vain in my heart,

To speak of him with my lips,

And to meet him in my dreams!

Yesterday the Eastern Pavilion was opened,

And my thoughts were all upon how the grand marriage would be arranged,

While, in a state of confused excitement, my mother told me to raise my green sleeves and to offer him cordially a jade cup of wine,

Which might have been regarded as a sign of her great affection for him,

But simply meant the ranking of me as his sister,

And making impossible our marriage.'

Hung Niang *says:*

Look, my Young Mistress, there is a halo round the moon. To-morrow, probably, it will be windy.

YING-YING *says:*

Yes, there is a halo round the moon.

She sings:

'When a mortal beauty is securely ensconced within the
embroidered curtains,

It is feared that she may be profaned by the touch of
man.

When I reflect that the Goddess of the Moon, rising in
the east and disappearing in the west, is unattended
and alone,

I feel displeased with the Lord of Heaven,

Who also allows not the lover to accompany his loved
one to fairyland,

And has taken the precaution to surround with a dense
curtain the Palace of the Moon,

For fear the heart of the Goddess might be moved to
love.'

(HUNG NIANG *coughs slightly.*)

MR. CHANG *says:*

That is Miss Hung Niang coughing. The Young
Lady has arrived. (*He plays on his lute.*)

YING-YING *says:*

Hung Niang, what is that sound?

HUNG NIANG *says:*

Guess, my Young Mistress.

YING-YING *sings:*

'Is it the tinkling sound of the head-ornaments as their
wearer walks?

Or is it the ringing sound of the ornaments of the skirt
as it sweeps along?

99

'THE SOUND IS GENTLE, LIKE FLOWERS

FALLING INTO RUNNING WATER'

Is it the creaking of the iron hinges as gusts of wind
    blow under the eaves?
Or is it the ding-dong sound of the gilt hooks knocking
    against the curtain frame?

Is it the evening bell that is being sounded in the
    Buddhist monastery?
Or is it the rustling sound of the few bamboos in the
    winding balustrade?
Is it the sound of the ivory foot-measure and the scissors
    that is wafted here?
Or is it the incessant dripping sound of the water-clock
    as the water falls into the copper receptacle?
Concealing myself, I listen again
At the eastern corner of the wall,
And find that it is indeed the sound of the strings of
    the lute coming from the Western Chamber.

The sound is powerful, like the sabres and spears of
    the mailed horsemen;
The sound is gentle, like flowers falling into running
    water;
The sound is high, like the cry of the crane at moon-
    light in the pure breeze;
The sound is low, like the whisper of lovers at the
    casement.

He is at his wits' end, but his sorrow is endless
Because he is separated from the young person he loves.
Before the tune is ended, already I realize its meaning,
Which distinctly expresses the separation of two love-
    birds.
It is entirely music without words!'

HUNG NIANG *says:*

> My Young Mistress, stay here to listen. I am
> going to see my Mistress and will return directly.
>
> (*She pretends to leave.*)

YING-YING *sings:*

'It is not because I have a good ear like any other
  person
That I know the feelings of your heart;
But because of the love we have for each other,
Which is affecting us with such pain and sorrow!'

MR. CHANG *says:*

> There is a slight sound outside the window. It
> must be the Young Lady. I will now try a tune.

YING-YING *says:*

> I must go nearer the window.

MR. CHANG *sighs and says:*

> Oh, my Lute! Formerly Ssu-ma Hsiang-ju, in
> wooing Cho Wên-chün, played a tune which was
> called the 'Phoenix Seeking his Mate'. How could
> I presume to call myself a second Hsiang-ju? But
> you, my Young Lady, how could Wên-chün com-
> pare in any way with you? I will now play this
> tune, following the original score. The tune
> says:

'There was once a fair lady, whom to see was never to
  forget.
Not to see her for a single day was to drive one to
  distraction.
The phoenix flies up and down, seeking everywhere his
  mate.

Alas! the fair lady is not by the eastern wall!
I play my lute to express my love;
When will you consent to my suit and relieve me from
    my anxiety?
My wish is to be united to one so perfect and, joined
    hand in hand, to be together for ever.
If I cannot fly with you as my companion, may I
    perish!'

YING-YING *says:*

How beautifully he plays! The song is so sad and
the tune so sorrowful that my eyes are filled with
tears without knowing it!

She sings:

'From beginning to end, there is a great variety of
    notes;
His song is neither like the sound of a bell in the silent
    night,
Nor like that of the weeping of Confucius at the sight
    of the unicorn,
Nor of the song about the unfortunate phoenix.

Word after word ripples as gently as the water from the
    water-clock that marks the night watches.
And sound after sound as sad as though uttered by one
    who is wasting away and finds his robe wide and
    his girdle loose.
The sorrow of estrangement and the grief of separation
Reveal themselves in this song,
And make me admire him more and more!'

MR. CHANG, *putting down the lute, says:*

Though your mother may be ungrateful and unjust, you, my Young Lady, should not prove to be a deceiver!

(HUNG NIANG *enters secretly*.)

YING-YING *says*:

Your plaint is unjustified!

She sings:

'That was a stratagem of my mother.
How can you say that I have deceived you?
She would not allow me to seek for a lover as a female
    phoenix seeks a male phoenix;
Night and day I have been forced to do nothing but
    needlework
And had no leisure whatever.
What cares she how others may implicate me?

Outside the window (where I am) is a curtain in the
    gentle breeze.
Inside, there is a lonely chamber (where he is) with a
    lamp alight.
Between us is only that window, on which is pasted a
    single sheet of red paper,
Which covers the openings of the lattice-work.
Though there are no cloudy mountains rising peak after
    peak (to divide us),
Still it is impossible to find an intermediary to convey
    my sentiments.
Formerly, even the Wu Mountain, with its twelve peaks,
Was celebrated as the land where the lover met the
    Goddess in his dream.'

HUNG NIANG *suddenly appears, and says*:

My Young Mistress, in what dream? If my Mistress gets to know this, what will happen?

YING-YING *sings:*

'She appears so hurriedly,
Regardless of my sorrow,
And has startled me and made me afraid.
I have never moved an inch.
Why does a mere chit like you speak in such a loud
    voice?
I must pat her and keep her here
In case she goes to my mother and thus makes an end
    of me.'

HUNG NIANG *says:*

I have just heard that Mr. Chang is going away.
My Young Mistress, what is to be done?

YING-YING *says:*

Hung Niang, you go and tell him to remain two
or three days longer.

She sings:

'You just say that my mother has now something to
    tell him,
And, good or bad, he will not go empty away.
Very cruel is my mother, who does not adhere to her
    words, ·
And is determined to separate me from my true and
    faithful lover.'

HUNG NIANG *says:*

My Young Mistress, it is unnecessary to give me
orders; I know how to act. I will go to-morrow
to see him.

[*Exeunt* YING-YING *and* HUNG NIANG.

MR. CHANG *says:*

> The Young Lady has gone. Miss Hung Niang,
> why did you not remain for a little longer, so that
> you might tell me to-night the response (of your
> Young Mistress to my music)? But things being
> as they are, all I can do is to go to sleep.   [*Exit.*

PART III

THE TITLES OF THE FOUR ACTS OF THE THIRD PART

CHANG CHÜN-JUI sends a love poem.

HUNG NIANG arranges a secret assignation.

TS'UI YING-YING assumes the part of a righteous judge.

MADAM inquires after MR. CHANG's health.

ACT I

FIRST EXPECTATIONS

YING-YING, *accompanied by* HUNG NIANG, *enters, and says:*

Since I heard the lute last night I have been feeling very uneasy to-day. Hung Niang, as you have nothing to do at the moment, you may as well go to the library to see Mr. Chang, hear what he has to say, and then come back and tell me.

HUNG NIANG *says:*

I will not go, for if my Mistress were to know, it would be no joke!

YING-YING *says:*

If I do not tell my mother, how will she know anything about it? You must go at once.

HUNG NIANG *says:*

Well, I will go. I will merely say to him: Mr. Chang, you have caused my Young Mistress a very great affliction.

'In the bright daylight, you and she have not yet drunk the cup of betrothal;

While in the chilly night she has to listen to the music of the lute!'

She sings:

'My Young Mistress has no heart to attend to her needle and thread;

The fragrant rouge and powder on her face have vanished and she has no inclination to renew them.

III

Her knitted eyebrows reveal her disappointed love.
If they could but see heart to heart,
The love-sickness which overwhelms her would be at
    once cured.'   [*Exit.*

YING-YING *says:*

    Hung Niang is gone. I must await her return to
    hear what she has to tell me.

'The many sentiments of my heart cannot be expressed
    in words;
All night long I think of him and during the day I am
    drowsy.'   [*Exit.*

MR. CHANG *enters, and says:*

    This will be my death! I requested the Superior
    to go to tell them that I am very seriously ill. Why
    is it they have not sent any one to visit me? Sad
    thoughts arise within me; I am so wearied, I will
    go and sleep for a little.

       (*He sleeps.*)

HUNG NIANG *enters, and says:*

    I have received the instructions of my Young
    Mistress to visit Mr. Chang, so I must go to carry
    them out. I reflect that if it were not for Mr.
    Chang, how could our family be still alive?

She sings:

'The coffin of the late Prime Minister, during its
    transportation,
Is temporarily resting in the lonely monastery.
A calamity has suddenly happened,
Which might have ended in my orphaned Young
    Mistress
Meeting her death at the hands of bandit soldiers.

Our thanks must be extended to Mr. Chang,
Who, by a letter, secured the sending of troops to rescue
  us promptly,
Truly it was the written word that saved the situation,
And had nothing to do with the so-called impartiality
  of Heaven and Earth.
If the five thousand bandits had not been wiped out,
  root and branch,
Is there any doubt but that the whole of the family
  would have been extinguished?
After having promised that Ying-ying and Chün-jui
  would become man and wife
Madam broke her word,
Putting him off with vain pretexts,
And the union was ruined
By the two lovers being styled mere brother and sister.
Now that the marriage has been entirely abandoned
The literary thoughts of the Scholar are thrown into
  confusion,
And the rouge and powder of the Beauty are bedewed
  with tears.

He, as handsome as P'an An, is so overcome with grief
  that his hair has turned grey;
While she, as Tu Wei Niang, is unlike her former fair
  self,
Her girdle becoming wider, and her figure slighter.
He, in a dazed condition, has lost his taste for reading
  his classics and histories,
While she, absent-minded, pays no attention to her
  embroidery.
He, on the strings of his lute, plays the tune revealing
  the sadness of separation,

While she, on the flowery paper, after revising and
    changing it, completes a poem on the Broken Heart.
The secret sentiments written by her pen,
And the love-strains from the strings of his lute,
Both show how mutually they love each other!

This, indeed, is a case of a great scholar and a beautiful
    maid!
I, Hung Niang, think to myself how peculiar human
    nature is!
Why should all with whom the course of true love never
    runs smooth act like this?
And have recourse to such eccentric acts?
If I were in the same case I would not think more than
    twice,
But accept my fate and end my life full of sadness!'

She says:

Here I am at last. Having wetted by licking it the
    paper covering the window, I will break it in order
    to see what he is doing in the library.

She sings:

'Having wetted and broken the paper covering the
    window,
I peep in silently.
It is probable that he has got up after having gone to
    bed with his clothes on.
Behold! the front of his silk gown is creased.
Alone he has slept.
Bitter and sad are his feelings:
He has no one to attend on him;
All his brightness has gone;
He breathes but feebly;

His cheeks are yellow and hollow.
Oh, Mr. Chang, if you do not die of sickness
You will certainly die of grief!
I will knock at the door with my gold hair-pin.

MR. CHANG *says:*

Who is there?

HUNG NIANG *sings:*

'I am the evil spirit of the five plagues, spreading abroad the microbes of love-sickness.'

>   (MR. CHANG *opens the door, and* HUNG NIANG *enters.*)

MR. CHANG *says:*

I am very grateful to you for the instruction you gave me last night. My gratitude is engraved on my heart, never to be forgotten. But I wonder whether your Young Mistress has had anything to say!

HUNG NIANG, *covering her mouth with her sleeve, laughs and says:*

My Young Mistress, I will tell you what she said.

She sings:

'Last evening, when the wind was fresh and the moon was bright and the night far advanced,
She ordered me to come to see you.
Up to this very moment she has neglected to rouge or powder her face;
And she has thought a thousand times of her lover as the highest scholar in the land.'

MR. CHANG *says:*

Since your Young Mistress shows so much love for me, Miss Hung Niang, I have a letter which I

should like to send to her. I think the best plan
would be to trouble you to take it for me.

HUNG NIANG *sings:*

'When she sees this poem, and the mode of its expression,
I warrant that she will really be beside herself with
delight.'

She says:

But she will pull a long face and say: Hung Niang,
from whom is this message that you have brought?

She sings:

' "You little minx! How dare you have such impu-
dence!"
The letter, torn up, falls in fragments.'

MR. CHANG *says:*

I am sure that your Young Mistress will not act like
this. It is only an excuse because you do not wish
to take the letter for me. I will give you, Miss
Hung Niang, a handsome monetary reward for
your trouble.

HUNG NIANG *sings:*

'You, Chang, are a wretched, poor, vulgar creature!
You want to make a show of how rich you are!
Do you think that I have come here to see what I can
get out of you?
How could all the salary that your wretched teaching
has earned be a sufficient reward for me!
Do you really believe that I want your money?

Do you think that people can be so easily moved as a
branch of peach or plum tree in the spring wind,

　Or can be purchased like those whose beauty is exposed
　　to the public?
　But I, though a mere servant-maid, have my dignity.
　If you were only to say, as you ought to: "Have pity
　　on me, a poor and lonely bachelor!"
　Then I would reconsider the matter.'

MR. CHANG *says:*

　As you say, Miss Hung Niang. Have pity on me,
　a poor and lonely bachelor! Will that do?

HUNG NIANG *says:*

　Yes, that is just it! Now write your letter and I
　will take it.

　　(MR. CHANG *writes.*)

HUNG NIANG *says:*

　How nice your handwriting looks! Read it to me
　so that I may hear what you have written.

MR. CHANG *reads, as follows:*

　Chang Kung salutes a hundred times and presents
　this letter to Miss Shuang Wên. The other day
　your honourable and kind mother rewarded my
　good services with unkindness, with the result that
　I felt more dead than alive. When the feast was
　over, sleep forsook me, so I played on my helpless
　lute to express my feelings and to indicate that
　henceforward both the lute and its player would
　be gone for ever! But, on account of the arrival
　of Hung Niang, I am sending you a few lines,
　hoping that you, who are so near and yet so far,
　may come to my rescue. Nothing is more precious
　than the life of man, so perhaps you will deign to
　take pity upon me. I will await the arrival of your
　decision in the greatest agitation. I add a poem
　which I hope you will condescend to read.

117

'When the sorrows of my love-sickness increased,
I took my lute and played on it as if at random.
Spring has come to welcome our happiness,
And has also moved your gentle heart.
The feelings of love cannot but be followed,
And vain advice should be disregarded.
We must not prove untrue to the brilliant moonlight,
But show our love where the beautiful flowers spread
    their shadows.'
    Chang Kung once more salutes a hundred times.

HUNG NIANG *sings:*

'I thought that you would carefully smooth the flowery
    paper in order to draft your letter,
But you have written it with a running pen without
    premeditation.
You have commenced it with merely conventional
    greetings,
And ended it by composing a poem of eight lines.
In a moment it has been folded up in the shape of a
    lover's knot.
You are very clever, exceedingly thoughtful, full of
    romance, and much of a gallant.
Although your behaviour as a lover may be a mere
    pretence,
No ordinary person could possibly act as you have done!

Your reversal of the order in which the characters for
    the love-birds are usually written,
Makes me now believe that you are as careful as you
    are thoughtful.
Whether the letter will cause anger or joy, I must watch
    her mood;
Make your mind easy on that score, Learned One!

I am only too pleased to do this for you
And have no thought of refusing.
I have also decided what to say.
All I will say is:
The lute-player of last night
Told me to deliver this letter.'

She says:

I will take this letter for you. But you, sir, ought
to bear in mind your career and maintain your
ambition.

She sings:

'The same hand that wishes to carry off the fair lady
Must be ready to pluck the cassia from the moon so
as to win the highest literary renown.
You must not profane your brilliant handwriting by
composing love-letters,
Nor let your very lofty flights of ambition be impeded
by love's entanglements;
Nor let your high purpose be destroyed by the sweet
song of a bird.
You must not, for the sake of a beauty ensconced within
her blue silk curtain,
Fail to attain the highest literary honours.

You have become as sick as Shên Yo,
And as sad as Sung Yü.
You seem to be wasting away through love-sickness.'

MR. CHANG *says:*

Miss Hung Niang, your kind words I will respect
and bear in mind for the rest of my life. But as
to that letter I just handed to you, my dear Miss
Hung Niang, you must be very careful.

HUNG NIANG *says:*

Make your mind easy, dear sir, on that score.

[*Exit.*

She sings:

'Even before the lovers' exchange of glances had revealed in full their love,

I have reflected in my heart, night and day, how to bring about the match.

How could I neglect such a precious letter as this?

I will most certainly have it delivered,

And with my own tongue I will speak,

And transmit the sentiments of love contained in the letter.

I warrant that I will make that person come to visit you at least once.'   [*Exit.*

MR. CHANG *says:*

Hung Niang has taken my letter. Without boasting, I say that it is a talisman which will effect our happy meeting. When she comes back with the answer to-morrow it will certainly be one of good news.

'If I had not availed of a favourable breeze to send a fine poem,

How could I expect a fairy, riding on the clouds, to come to visit me in my dreams?'   [*Exit.*

ACT II

THE FUSS ABOUT THE BILLET-DOUX

YING-YING *enters, and says:*

> I expect Hung Niang may arrive at any moment. As I got up earlier this morning than usual, I will now go to sleep again for a little.
>
> (*She sleeps.*)

HUNG NIANG *enters, and says:*

> By the order of my Young Mistress, I went to see Mr. Chang and have brought back a letter. I must now report to her. Ah! I don't hear a single sound of her. She has probably gone to sleep again. I must go in to see her.

> 'The sun, as it slowly rises, lightens the green-curtained window,
> The swallows, in pairs, fly to and fro in the quiet spring air.'

She sings:

> 'The curtains hang still in the wind.
> From the window, covered with gauze, is spread around a fragrance of lily and musk,
> When I open the red doors the two copper rings resound.
> On a high, red stand are the small lilies, yellow as gold.
> The light of the silver lamp is still bright.
> I gently draw aside her warm curtains
> And lift up the red silk valance to have a peep at her.

'I SEE HER JADE HAIR-PIN, NOT PROPERLY FIXED, SLANTING

'DOWNWARDS, AND HER CLOUDS OF HAIR ARE ALL DISHEVELLED'

I see her jade hair-pin, not properly fixed, slanting
    downwards,
And her clouds of hair are all dishevelled.
Although the sun is high in the sky, her eyes are still
    closed.
You are indeed lazy, very lazy!'

> (YING-YING *rises, stretches herself, and sighs
>   deeply.*)

'After some time, sitting up,
And scratching her ears several times,
She heaves a deep sigh.'

HUNG NIANG *says:*

> This being the situation, how can I deliver the
> letter to my Young Mistress? My best plan will
> be to place it in her toilet case and wait till she sees
> it herself.

> (*She places it there.*)

> (YING-YING *makes her toilet.*   HUNG NIANG
>   *furtively looks at her.*)

HUNG NIANG *sings:*

'Her rouge and powder of the previous night having
    faded,
And her black clouds of hair having fallen down,
She slightly powders her face
And carelessly arranges her locks.
She takes up the letter
And then puts the toilet case down.
Opening the envelope, she reads its contents most
    intently.
She peruses the letter over and over again without
    showing any signs of weariness.

Then I see her knit her black eyebrows with an air of
  displeasure
And suddenly bend her head, showing her white neck,
When her fair face immediately changes to one of
  anger.'

She, first revealing by dumb show her views, says:
  Alas! the game is up!

YING-YING, *in anger, says:*
  Come here, Hung Niang!

HUNG NIANG *says:*
  I am here.

YING-YING *says:*

  Hung Niang, where has this thing come from? I
  am the daughter of the late Prime Minister. Who
  dares to make a sport of me with such letters as
  this? When have I ever been accustomed to read
  such a thing as this? I am going to tell my mother
  about it so that she may give you, little imp, a
  good thrashing!

HUNG NIANG *says:*

  It was you, my Young Mistress, who sent me to
  him and he who sent me back with the letter. If
  you, my Young Mistress, had not sent me to him,
  how could I have dared to ask him for it? Besides,
  I cannot read, so how could I know what he has
  written?

She sings:

  'It is quite clear that the fault is yours.
  And now, without rhyme or reason, I am to be the
    injured victim.

You want to make others suffer unjustly for what you
    have done!
You say you have not been accustomed to such things,
    but who has been accustomed?

She says:

My Young Mistress, do not make so much fuss!
Rather than you should tell your mother about this,
let me take the letter to her and be the first to act
as an informer.

YING-YING, *in anger, says:*

When you go to my mother, against whom will
you inform?

HUNG NIANG *says:*

Against Mr. Chang.

YING-YING, *first revealing by dumb show her sentiments,*
says:

Hung Niang, stay your hand, and pardon him this
time.

HUNG NIANG *says:*

My Young Mistress, is it not probable that he will
be given a good thrashing?

YING-YING *says:*

I have not yet asked you how fares Mr. Chang's
sickness.

HUNG NIANG *says:*

I shall not tell you.

YING-YING *says:*

Oh, Hung Niang, do tell me!

HUNG NIANG *sings:*

'Recently his face has become so thin as to be almost
  unbearable to look at;
He has no desire either to eat or to drink,
And fears to make the slightest movement.'

YING-YING *says:*

A doctor of highest skill must be called in to
examine his sickness.

HUNG NIANG *says:*

He has no special sickness.   He himself said:

She sings:

'Night and day, I am looking forward to the happy
  meeting.
I have abandoned my sleep and forgotten my meals.
From eve till morn my eyes, filled with tears, gaze at
  the Eastern Wall (where dwells my beloved).
The only cure for my sickness
Is to have some romantic excitements!'

YING-YING *says:*

Fortunately, you have always been discreet of
speech, for if others know of this what will become
of the honour of our family?   From now henceforward, if he makes use of such language as this,
you must never mention it.   The relations between
Mr. Chang and myself are merely those of brother
and sister, and nothing more.

HUNG NIANG *says:*

Those are very fine words!

She sings:

'If you are afraid that his flirting with you will lead to
  harm,

And that it will be discovered by your mother sooner
or later,
How can either you or I feel anything but uneasiness?
Why should you care whether his sickness is dangerous
or not?
What you have done is simply to encourage him to
climb up,
And then, having removed the ladder, to pretend to
regard him with indifference.

YING-YING *says:*

Although our family is under obligation to him,
how can he be allowed to act like this? Hand me
pen and paper so that I may write an answer to
him, telling him that he must not act in this manner
again.

HUNG NIANG *says:*

My Young Mistress, why should you write? Why
should you trouble yourself like this?

YING-YING *says:*

Hung Niang, you don't understand!
(*She writes.*)

She says:

Hung Niang, you take this letter and say to him:
'When my Young Mistress last sent me to see you,
sir, that was simply a matter of courtesy between
a sister and a brother and had no other meaning.
But if you repeat what you have done, she will
certainly tell her mother.' And you, Hung Niang,
you little imp, will also have to answer for this!

HUNG NIANG *says:*

My Young Mistress, you are fussing again! I will
not take your letter. Why should you trouble
yourself like this?

YING-YING, *throwing the letter on the ground, says:*
　　What an ignoramus this little chit is!　　[*Exit.*

HUNG NIANG, *picking up the letter, sighs and says:*
　　Ah! My Young Mistress, why do you show such
　　temper?

She sings:

'Young maidens know not how to restrain their lan-
　　guage,
And are always only too ready to abuse others.
If you show such bad temper,
You must give up all thoughts of your beloved Scholar,
And thus show yourself a model for all maidens of good
　　families to follow!

In my dreams I dreamt that you two were united,
But when I awoke you were single once more.
For your sake I have abandoned sleep and forgotten
　　to eat;
And even my silk robe did not prevent me feeling cold
　　during the small hours of the morning.
My grief for you was without limit;
And silently my tears kept falling from my eyes.

As long deferred as the rising of the planet Mercury,
Is that happy union for which I have long hoped in vain.
I have never shut the side door,
Wishing that you might become husband and wife
Without any danger or difficulty,
And that you, in full bridal array, would appear at the
　　wedding-feast,
While I keep my lips sealed as to my role of inter-
　　mediary.

When making your toilet in your boudoir at night, after
the spring flowers had fallen,
You were afraid that your garments were too thin to
keep out the cold.
But on the evening when you heard the sound of the lute
And the heavy dew sparkled in the bright moonlight,
Why did you not fear the cold of spring that night?
Was it because you were devoured by the passion for
that scholar?
At that time did you not feel ashamed
Of your feelings for that wretched, sour, crazy fellow,
As you looked so longingly for him through the window,
resembling her who was turned to stone as she
awaited her husband?

Since you have revealed your desire to make love
I have been ready to show my goodwill to act as bearer
of your missives.
Unwilling to dwell on your own rash folly,
You show yourself only too prompt to find fault with
others.
I will, for the time, put up with this injustice, as one who
has to bear painful treatment like the cauterizing
by moxa.
Crafty indeed you are!
In public you are full of plausible speeches and flowery
words,
But in private your eyebrows are knit in sorrow and
your eyes are filled with tears.'

She says:

If I don't go with the letter of my Young Mistress
she will say that I have disobeyed her orders.
Besides, Mr. Chang is waiting for me to bring an

answer. There is therefore nothing for me but to return to the library.

(*She knocks at the door.*)

MR. CHANG *says:*

So you have come, Miss Hung Niang. What about the letter?

HUNG NIANG *says:*

It has failed. Don't be silly, sir.

MR. CHANG *says:*

My letter was a talisman to effect a happy meeting, but you have not acted with sufficient zeal, so that the result is like this.

HUNG NIANG *says:*

Do you say that I have been wanting in zeal, sir? Heaven alone knows the truth! The contents of your letter were anything but good!

She sings:

'It is because your luck is bad,
And not because I have been neglectful!
That letter of yours is your confession,
Is a summons for you to appear,
And a proof that I am concerned in the case.
If she had not a friendly regard for me,
And was willing to pardon your rash impertinence.
I should have been held as guilty.

From now henceforward visits will be rare and meetings
     will be difficult;
The moon will no longer shine on the Western Chamber;
The phoenix will leave the Pavilion of Ch'in for ever;
And the clouds will disappear from the Wu Mountains.

131

You will take the high road and I will take the low road;
And I request you, sir, to drop the subject.
Let us depart at once, for when the feast is over the
guests disperse.'

She says:

This is the end of the matter. You, sir, need not
trouble again to reveal your inmost sentiments.
My Mistress may be looking for me, so I must
return at once!

Mr. CHANG *says:*

Miss Hung Niang! (*He remains motionless.*)

After a long time Mr. CHANG, *weeping, says:*

Miss Hung Niang, once you have gone who is
there with whom I can expect to plead my cause?

Mr. CHANG, *kneeling down, says:*

Miss Hung Niang! Miss Hung Niang! You must
really help to have this matter put right for me,
and thus save my life.

HUNG NIANG *says:*

You are a very learned scholar, sir. Can you not
understand how the matter really stands?

She sings:

'Do not show your cunning by playing the fool!
While you want to have the full enjoyment of your
love-affair
You will cruelly cause my flesh and bones to suffer
torture.
For my Young Mistress, brandishing a rod in her hands,
would be ready to beat me.
The whole matter is as impossible as for a thick rope
to go through the eye of a needle.

Do you want me to act as a go-between when I may
    have to support myself with a staff (owing to my
    having been beaten)?

How can I act as such when I have to keep my lips
    sealed?

I have already risked too much on your behalf!'

MR. CHANG, *still kneeling and weeping, says:*

There is no other way for me. The only hope of
    saving my life depends on you, Miss Hung Niang!

HUNG NIANG *sings:*

'But now I cannot resist the charming effect of your
    honeyed words,

Which places me in a great dilemma!'

She says:

I cannot find words to explain my difficulties.
    Here is the answer to your letter from my Young
    Mistress, which you can read for yourself. (*She
    hands him the letter.*)

MR. CHANG, *having opened and read the letter, gets up and
    smilingly says:*

Ah, Miss Hung Niang!

He reads again and says:

To-day is indeed a happy day!

He reads again and says:

Had I known before that your Young Mistress' letter
    was to arrive, I should have prepared for its recep-
    tion in a proper manner. Now it is too late for
    that so I hope I may be excused. Miss Hung
    Niang, I feel sure you will rejoice!

HUNG NIANG *says:*

What about?

MR. CHANG *smilingly says:*

> The abuse of me by your Young Mistress is all put on! In the letter she says 'so and so', and 'so and so'!

HUNG NIANG *says:*

> Really?

MR. CHANG *says:*

> In her letter she makes an assignation with me to go to the garden to-night.

HUNG NIANG *says:*

> An assignation to go to the garden? What for?

MR. CHANG *says:*

> To go to the garden to meet each other!

HUNG NIANG *says:*

> To meet each other! What for?

MR. CHANG *smilingly says:*

> For what do you think we are going to meet, Miss Hung Niang?

HUNG NIANG *says:*

> I simply cannot believe it!

MR. CHANG *says:*

> You may believe it or not as you like.

HUNG NIANG *says:*

> Let me hear you read it.

MR. CHANG *says:*

> It is a poem of four lines with five characters each. It is beautiful.

'Await in the moonlight at the Western Chamber,
Where the door stands half opened by the breeze.

While the shadows of the flowers move on the wall,
The Precious One may be coming!'

Are you still incredulous, Miss Hung Niang?

HUNG NIANG *says:*

What is the explanation of this?

MR. CHANG *says:*

What is there to explain?

HUNG NIANG *says:*

I really cannot understand.

MR. CHANG *says:*

Well, then, I will explain it to you. 'Await in the
moonlight at the Western Chamber' means that I
must be there when the moon rises. 'Where the
door stands half opened by the breeze' means that
she will open the door and wait for me. 'While
the shadows of the flowers move on the wall'
means that I am to climb over the wall. 'The
Precious One may be coming' should not be inter-
preted literally, as it means, 'I am coming.'

HUNG NIANG *says:*

Is this really the explanation?

MR. CHANG *says:*

If it is not to be explained as I have done, Miss
Hung Niang, let me hear your explanation! I
would not dare to deceive you, Miss Hung Niang.
I am a past master in the art of solving poetical
riddles, full of romance like Sui Ho, and a born
gallant like Lu Chia! If it is not to be explained
as I have done, how is it to be explained then?

HUNG NIANG *says:*

Is it really written in that way?

135

MR. CHANG *says:*

> Here it is.

>> (HUNG NIANG *remains motionless for a long time.*)

>> (MR. CHANG *reads it again.*)

HUNG NIANG *says:*

> Is it really written in that way?

MR. CHANG *smilingly says:*

> Miss Hung Niang, you are too absurd! Here it is!

HUNG NIANG *angrily says:*

> So my Young Mistress has made a fool of me!

She sings:

> 'Who has ever seen a messenger, sent with a letter, so thoroughly befooled by the sender?
> Young though my Young Mistress may be, her mind is very crafty!
> Telling you, her lover, to jump over the Eastern Wall, she wishes to carry on an intrigue with you,
> As the poem hints, at the hour of midnight,
> And at the trysting-place.
> At the critical moment, you betray me!
> Wishing to carry on your love-affair, you select a retired spot in the crowded monastery;
> And you want me to find time to take your letter, busy though I am!

> Brilliant and smooth as jade was the paper.
> The writing exhaled a fragrance like that of lily and musk.

The lines were wet not with the moisture of her beautiful person,
But bedewed throughout with tears of blood caused by
her feelings of love,
And the ink of the whole letter remained as melancholy
wet as the rainy spring.
From henceforward, you may banish all doubts.
And you, who have attained high literary renown, may
make your mind easy
As to obtaining possession at will of the young maiden
with the gold bird in her hair.

To him you have shown special affection,
But me you have disregarded.
I wonder when have you become his respectful wife!
To him you have used honeyed, flattering words, which
would make one warm even in mid-winter,
But to me you have spoken harsh and cruel words,
which would make one cold even in midsummer!
From to-day I will keep a watch on you, my bewitching
young beauty,
And see what steps you take to attract your handsome
lover.'

MR. CHANG *says:*

How can a student like myself climb over a garden
wall?

HUNG NIANG *sings:*

'The flowers that brush against the wall are not high,
And the door in the breeze is only half closed.
The attempt to steal the scented lady must now be
made by you!
If you are afraid of the height of the wall, how will you
be able to jump over the Dragon's Gate?

And if the mass of the flowers deters you, how will you
    ever be able to pluck the cassia of the Immortals?
Make all haste and have no fear!
Her eyes, dark as the waves of autumn, stand out with
    expectancy,
And her eyebrows, delicate as the outline of the hills
    in spring, are knit in sorrow.'

MR. CHANG *says:*

    I have already visited the garden twice.

HUNG NIANG *sings:*

    'Although you have been there twice,
    This visit is not likely to be the same.
    Formerly your interchange of poetry, with the wall
        between you, was mere by-play,
    But her letter of to-day is the proof of the real thing!'
                                                 [*Exit.*

MR. CHANG *says:*

    Alas, all things are fated! When Hung Niang
    arrived just now I was depressed beyond words.
    But who could have thought that the Young Lady
    would give me such happiness! I am indeed a
    past master in the art of solving poetical riddles,
    am full of romance like Sui Ho and a born gallant
    like Lu Chia. If these four lines of the poem are
    not to be explained in this way, how are they to
    be explained? 'Await in the moonlight at the
    Western Chamber' must mean to await the rise of
    the moon; 'Where the door stands half opened by
    the breeze', then the door must be open; 'While
    the shadows of the flowers move on the wall the
    Precious One may be coming.' When the shadows
    of the flowers are on the wall it will be the time
    for me to go. To-day the wretched daylight seems

to be endless.   Oh, Heaven! you, on whose universal bounty we depend, why are you so cruel as to begrudge me this day?   Let the sun quickly sink!

'A happy letter comes from a happy friend with happy words,
And the sun sinks imperceptibly in the west and darkness supervenes.
But to-day, when I have a meeting where the peach blossoms grow,
The sun seems glued and rooted in the sky!'

It is now midday!   I must still wait a while before I look again.   To-day everything seems against the sun's setting!

'The blue vault of the firmament is cloudless.
A delicate fragrance is wafted from afar by the breeze.
Where can be found the secret for shortening the day,
And for making the sun sink in the west?'

Ah!   It is beginning to sink in the west!   Again I must wait a while.

'Who put that three-legged bird
In Heaven's high palace?
How can I secure the bow of Hou I
To shoot down the bright disk?'

Thanks to Heaven and thanks to Earth, you, the God of the Sun's brightness, are bound to disappear at the fixed time!   Ah!   The lamps are already being lighted!   Ah!   The drums of the first watch are being beaten!   Ah!   The evening bells already are sounding!   I close the door of the library and go there.   I clasp the branches of the drooping willow and in a trice jump over the wall.

139

I hold in my embrace the Young Lady! Oh, my Young Lady! How sad I feel on your account!

'The twenty words of the poetical message are as precious as twenty pearls,
And our union, predestined three thousand years, is to be fulfilled in the flower-garden.'   [*Exit*.

ACT III

REPUDIATION OF THE BILLET-DOUX

HUNG NIANG *enters, and says:*

> To-day my Young Mistress, when ordering me to take what she had written to Mr. Chang, assumed in my presence an entirely false attitude, while in the poem she actually made a secret assignation with him. As my Young Mistress said nothing to me about it I will not give her away, but will simply ask her to come to burn incense; and I should like to see how she can humbug me when the critical moment arrives.

She respectfully says:

> My Young Mistress, let us go to burn incense.

YING-YING *enters, and says:*

> 'How very sweet is the fragrance of the flower in the gentle evening breeze,
> While the bright moon rises early over the courtyard, where profound silence reigns!'

HUNG NIANG *sings:*

> 'Cold and penetrating is the evening breeze which comes through the gauze-covered window.
> The embroidered curtain, with its gilt hooks attached, has not yet been hung up.
> The evening vapours collect around the entrance and the veranda of the garden.

The red rays of the setting sun colour the kiosk and
the pavilion.
My Young Mistress, in front of her mirror, has just
finished her evening toilet in her boudoir.

Far removed from noise and bustle,
The ducks sleep on the light green water of the pond.
A scene as natural as it is tranquil and beautiful is
The pale yellow willow on which are perched the crows.
With her small feet she crushes the young shoots of the
peony,
And her jade hair-ornament is entangled in the red
flowers supported by a framework.
The moss that covers the path is slippery;
The pearls of dew soak her stockings as she gracefully
sails along.'

She says:

It seems to me that my Young Mistress and Mr.
Chang can scarcely restrain themselves until the
night arrives.

She sings:

'Ever since the rising of the sun they have been longing
for the brilliant moon.
To them a moment has seemed an age!
When they saw the sun slowly sinking behind the tops
of the willows,
They said, "Would that the Holy Ones would make it
vanish for ever!"

Bewitchingly arrayed,
She is fully prepared to meet her lover in the valley of
the Wu Mountains.

She longs to mate with him in the manner of the
  swallows and orioles;
And, having lost her heart, she is full of restlessness.
Neither drink nor food touches her lips.
As formerly she was so bashful and retiring,
It is difficult to say whether that demeanour was
  genuine or assumed.
For now she is unable to restrain her passion,
And is acting altogether without any sense of propriety!'

She says:

My Young Mistress, stand here below this rock,
and I will shut the side door, lest some one might
overhear what we are saying.

MR. CHANG *enters, and says:*

This is just the right time to go there.

(*He looks inside the door.*)

HUNG NIANG *sings:*

'It seems to be the crows in the *Sophora japonica* which
  throws its shadow as it is rocked in the evening
  breeze,
But it is really the handsome Scholar wearing his black
  silk head-dress slightly on one side.
On the one hand, he conceals himself behind the
  balustrade in the winding passage,
While on the other she stands with her back to the rock.
This is no place for ordinary conventional conversation,
And they do not interchange a word.'

MR. CHANG, *embracing* HUNG NIANG, *says:*

My dear Young Lady!

HUNG NIANG *says:*

You beast! It is I! Luckily the mistake has been

'THE BRANCHES OF WEEPING WILLOW AND THE FLOWERS ACT AS CURTAINS;

'AND THE GREEN MOSS SERVES AS A SPACIOUS AND EMBROIDERED COUCH!'

made with me; supposing it had been made with
my Mistress, what would have happened?

She sings:

'Although the embrace may be due to excitement,
You ought to look before you embrace!
Probably this is owing to your extreme hunger causing
you to see stars.'

She says:

Let me ask you if you have been really told to
come here.

MR. CHANG *says:*

I am a past master in the art of solving poetical
riddles, full of romance like Sui Ho and a born
gallant like Lu Chia! So I am quite certain that I
will completely captivate her.

HUNG NIANG *says:*

Don't go through the door or she will say that I
have let you in. You must jump over the wall.
Don't you see, Mr. Chang? This evening, with
its beautiful surroundings, is evidently assisting
you and her to complete your union.

She sings:

'Behold, a slight cloud veils the brightness of the moon,
Just like a shade of red paper surrounding a silver
candlestick.
The branches of weeping willow and the flowers act as
curtains;
And the green moss serves as a spacious and embroidered couch!

The beautiful night is far advanced,
And profound silence reigns in the empty court.

The branches of the flowers are weighed down by
blossoms.

But you must realize that she is an innocent young
maiden,

Whom you must treat with great gentleness,

Address with caressing words,

And whose affections you can only win by a sweet
disposition.

Do not for a moment imagine that she is like a roadside
willow or a broken blossom.

Her delicate beauty is as full of grace as jade without
flaw.

Behold, how full her fair face is of attractive charm!

And how her raven locks are waved like clouds!

No longer will I have to expose myself to fear or alarms

Or to hope for a cup of cheap wine or tea as reward.

I take pity on you, because when you lie down to sleep
under your coverlet

You have no one except yourself to comfort you.

Brace yourself up,

End your anxiety,

Banish your sorrow and grief,

And prepare to show yourself to be a man of understanding!'

(MR. CHANG *jumps over the wall.*)

YING-YING *says:*

Who is it?

MR. CHANG *says:*

It is I.

YING-YING *calls:*

Hung Niang!   Hung Niang!

(*There is no reply.*)

147

YING-YING *angrily says:*
> Oh, oh, Mr. Chang! What kind of a man are you?
> While I am burning incense here, you have come
> without rhyme or reason. What explanation have
> you to offer?

MR. CHANG, *surprised, says:*
> Ah!

HUNG NIANG *sings:*
> 'When is a go-between free from alarm and fear?
> When those who are to become devoted husband and
>   wife have no idea of difference or quarrel.
> I must go on tiptoe and furtively, to listen secretly to
>   them:
> One of whom is full of shame,
> And the other is full of anger!
> One has no word to say,
> While the other has changed her mind!
> One is absolutely silent and deeply depressed,
> While the other is chattering endlessly!'

She, standing at a distance, says in a low voice:
> Mr. Chang, what has become of all your bold talk
> behind her back? Go on! If this matter is re-
> ported to the authorities, do you think you will be
> the only one to be disgraced?

She sings:
> 'Why has the romantic Sui Ho been so suddenly
>   checked?
> And why has the gallant Lu Chia been so speedily
>   silenced?
> Standing there, with clasped hands and bowing body,
> You look as if you are deaf and dumb!

148

When there is no one present, your tongue wags easily.
Your cunning and craftiness are mere make-believe.
Who would have thought that your demeanour by
the rock would be so different from that in the
Western Chamber?'

YING-YING *says:*

Hung Niang, there is a thief here!

HUNG NIANG *says:*

Who is it, my Young Mistress?

MR. CHANG *says:*

It is I, Miss Hung Niang.

HUNG NIANG *says:*

Who told you to come here, Mr. Chang, and what
is your business in coming here?

(MR. CHANG *maintains silence.*)

YING-YING *says:*

Drag him off at once to where my mother is!

(MR. CHANG *still maintains silence.*)

HUNG NIANG *says:*

If we drag him off to where my Mistress is it will
ruin his reputation. Let me deal with him for
you, my Young Mistress. Mr. Chang, come here
and kneel down. Since you have read the books
of Confucius, you should thoroughly understand
the proper ways of behaviour as laid down by
Duke Chou. What have you come here for at this
late hour of night?

She sings:

'This fine pumpkin is now in the hands of a fair sweet
maiden!

149

It is not that we wish to pose as judges,
But we wish to give you some heartfelt, good advice.
I simply regarded you as possessed of a scholarship
      profound as the sea,
But who would have thought that your audacity,
      prompted by your heart, would be as unlimited as
      the heavens?
You, who have come late at night to our house,
Are liable to be arrested if not as an abductor, then as
      a robber!
You, who are attempting to attain the highest literary
      honours by plucking the cassia from the Moon,
Have become the seductive tempter of the fair sex.
Instead of becoming a renowned scholar by jumping
      over the Dragon Gate,
Your jump over the garden wall is as simple as mounting
      a horse!'

She says:
> My Young Mistress, for my sake, please forgive
> him.

YING-YING *says:*
> To your kindness, sir, we are indebted for our
> lives, and we are bound to repay that kindness.
> But since we have become brother and sister, how
> can you have such a desire? Should my mother
> by any chance know of this, how could you possibly
> feel at ease? Now, for the sake of Hung Niang, I
> will forgive you this time. But should it occur
> again you will be dragged to where my mother is,
> and that will not be the end of the matter!

HUNG NIANG *sings:*
> 'Thanks to the wisdom and the prudence of my Young
> Mistress

You have been pardoned for my sake.
Had the case gone before the authorities for full investigation,
You, sir, would have had to prepare for receiving a severe beating upon your delicate skin!'

YING-YING *says:*

Hung Niang, remove the table for burning incense and come in with me.   [*Exit.*

HUNG NIANG, *mocking* MR. CHANG, *says:*

For shame! For shame! Did you not say that you were a past master in the art of solving poetical riddles, full of romance like Sui Ho and a born gallant like Lu Chia? From to-day you may regard all your schemes as being as good as dead!

She sings:

'Speak no more of that night of love, one moment of which was worth a thousand pieces of gold,
But prepare yourself for a single life of ten years more in your lonely study!
You, the past master in the art of solving poetical riddles, made a mistake in knocking at the door, which stood half opened by the breeze;
Now there is an obstacle as high as a mountain instead of mere shadows of the flowers moving on the wall;
And the moonlight awaiting at the Western Chamber is hidden in clouds!
Beautify yourself as much as you like, as did Mr. Ho of old;
But she prefers to paint her own eyebrows without your playing the part of Chang Ch'ang.
You, poor wretch, with a forced attempt at romance,

Are like a threatening storm of cloud and rain, resulting
    in a drought!
Your audacity in trying to make love to the fair lady
    should now be a source of regret to you,
And your gallant speeches to your beloved one should
    be entirely forgotten!
Cease at once your seductive poems,
And from henceforward write no more letters.
You are still a tyro in the art of romance.
You, my Young Mistress, like the heroine, Cho Wên-
    chün, be angry no more.
And you, Mr. Chang, like the lovesick hero, Ssŭ-ma
    Hsiang-ju, go and continue your studies!'

[*Exeunt.*

ACT IV

FURTHER EXPECTATIONS

MADAM *enters, and says:*

> Early this morning the Superior sent a messenger
> to tell me that Mr. Chang was very ill. I therefore
> sent a skilled doctor and at the same time ordered
> Hung Niang to go to see him, to inquire what
> medicine he had prescribed, what the malady is,
> what is the condition of his pulse, and to bring me
> back an answer at once. [*Exit.*

HUNG NIANG *enters, and says:*

> My Mistress has sent me to see Mr. Chang. Oh!
> my Mistress! all you know is that Mr. Chang is
> very ill. How could you possibly know that he
> met last night with such a rebuff? I fear that it
> may cause his death! [*Exit.*

YING-YING *enters, and says:*

> Mr. Chang is very ill, so I have written a missive
> to him, which, as I shall tell Hung Niang when
> ordering her to take it, is only a prescription, but
> will give him reassurance. (*She calls.*)

HUNG NIANG *answers:*

> I am coming, my Young Mistress.

YING-YING *says:*

> Mr. Chang is very ill. I have an excellent pre-
> scription, which you must take to him for me.

HUNG NIANG *says:*

> Oh, Young Mistress, you are at it again! Very

well, as my Mistress has just ordered me to go to him, I will take it for you.

YING-YING *says:*

I will make a point of waiting till you return with an answer.   [*Exeunt.*

MR. CHANG *enters, and says:*

Last night, in the garden, I met with such a serious rebuff that it has brought on my old malady. It is obvious that I am done for. Madam has told the Superior to call in a skilled doctor to see me, but as my dangerous malady is not one that any skilled doctor can deal with, it is only some good prescription of the Young Lady that can cure it.

HUNG NIANG *enters, and says:*

My Young Mistress, having caused him a terrible sickness, has now ordered me to take a prescription, goodness knows of what kind. Of course I will go, but I only fear it will make him still worse.

'In a strange land, home-sickness most easily arises;
The finest medicine cannot heal a broken heart!'

She sings:

'You were the first, with your flowery pen, to write a love poem,
As ornamental as an embroidered palindrome,
Which had the effect of preventing him from raising his head from his pillow in his bed,
And of making him forgetful of his food and unable to rest in peace.
So now his locks are as grey as those of the sorrowful P'an,
And his figure is as wasted as that of the sick Shên.

His regret is as profound as his sickness is serious,
Owing to your having violently rebuffed him to his face,
And to your having wounded him with your icy words!

You stood on the threshold, awaiting the rising of the
  moon;
You composed your love poem to rhyme with his;
And listened with ear intent to the playing of the lute.'

She says:

But last night you suddenly talked a lot of nonsense, saying: 'Mr. Chang, you and I are related
as brother and sister. What has brought you here?'

She sings:

'And quite unexpectedly you have entrapped the
Scholar!'

She says:

To-day you say: 'Hung Niang, I have an excellent
prescription which you must take and give to him.'

She sings:

'The manner in which I, your handmaid, am oppressed
is unbearable!
I am kept going perpetually, just like the thread which
never leaves the needle.
From henceforth let things go as they may!
The so-called good faith as profound as the sea and
kindness as high as the hills
Are nothing more than the distant water and the elusive
peak which are never reached!'

She sees MR. CHANG *and questions him:*

I feel very sorry for you, Mr. Chang. How is your
health to-day?

155

MR. CHANG *says:*

> It will be the death of me! Should I die, Miss Hung Niang, you must be my witness at the tribunal of the King of Hades.

HUNG NIANG *says:*

> Many people in this world suffer from love-sickness, but no one is so seriously affected by it as you. Oh, my Young Mistress, how can you realize his suffering!

She sings:

> 'Your mind no longer dwells on the vast sea of learning and the wide forest of literature;
> You dream of nothing but the shade of the willows and the shadow of the flowers where lovers meet,
> Your heart being bent on secret meetings with the fair one.
> But all so far has been in vain,
> Though I have seen that your loving thoughts of her have been continued since the begonia first bloomed in spring.'

She says:

> How is it that you are suffering to such an extent?

MR. CHANG *says:*

> How could I dare to lie in your presence! It is because of your Young Mistress. Last night, when I was sent back to the library, I was beside myself with anger. I, the saviour, have been wronged by her whom I saved. The old saw says: 'A doting maid and an unfaithful swain', but to-day the case is reversed.

HUNG NIANG *says:*

> But she is really not to blame for this.

She sings:

> 'Examine yourself and your improper desires!
> Look at yourself, reduced to a mere skeleton by that
>> devil of a complaint that has attacked you!
> You may excuse yourself by saying that such has ever
>> been the fate of the scholar.
> But such one-sided love is better ended without more
>> ado.
> On the one hand, your literary ambition has failed;
> On the other, your matrimonial attempts have only led
>> to endless murmurings.'

She says:

> My Mistress has ordered me to come to see what
> medicine you are taking, but there is another
> excellent prescription—goodness knows what it is
> —which I have brought to give to you.

MR. CHANG *says:*

> Where is it?

HUNG NIANG *hands it to him, and says:*

> Here it is.

MR. CHANG *opens and reads it. He stands up and smilingly
says:*

> I am more than delighted! It is a poem.

He bows and says:

> Had I known before that this was a poem from
> your Young Mistress I should have been bound
> to receive it on my knees. Oh! Miss Hung
> Niang, my poor health has suddenly and im-
> perceptibly quite disappeared.

HUNG NIANG *says:*

> You are at it again! But don't make any mistake
> this time!

157

MR. CHANG *says:*

> Where did I make a mistake? Last night there
> was no mistake in what I did. Success or failure
> is a mere matter of chance.

HUNG NIANG *says:*

> I don't believe it. You read the poem to me.

MR. CHANG *says:*

> If you want to hear the excellent words, you must
> come forward and with the utmost respect make
> your bow.

MR. CHANG *adjusts his hat and girdle, and, holding the poem
with both hands, reads:*

> 'Trouble not your heart with mere trifles,
> And destroy not the talents with which Heaven has
> endowed you.
> Little did I think that, by maintaining my maidenly
> modesty,
> It would prove such a calamity to you.
> In order to repay your great kindness, it is impossible
> to act with the usual proprieties,
> So I present you with a new poem to serve as a medium.
> These words I send to my lover, who need not respond
> in verse.
> For to-night, without fail, my lover, I will come to
> you!'

> Miss Hung Niang, this poem cannot be compared
> with that of yesterday.

HUNG NIANG, *bending her head and reflecting, says:*

> Oh! That is it! Now I understand! My Young
> Mistress, your prescription is indeed a good one!

She sings:

'When the cassia flowers throw their shadow and the
    night is far advanced,
The poor Scholar, who should retire to rest,
Remains in the shadow of the rocks to seize a chance
    that may never recur,
Of which he may avail himself once and again as he
    pleases.
But it is feared that the all-knowing mother is not yet
    asleep,
Or that Hung Niang may play false.
These circumstances should make a gentleman a little
    reflective.

You are only a fool, so do not try to look wise.
A crazy scholar, as you certainly are,
Knows not where to seek for good news,
So tries to discover it in this missive.
And having received this bit of paper, you are making
    much ado about nothing.
But when you saw the Heavenly One,
Why did you prove so helplessly weak?
It is only natural that my Young Mistress is unmindful
    of your former kindness,
And is as ungrateful as a beggar!

You sleep under a coverlet of ordinary stuff,
And use as your pillow your three-foot long lute.
When she comes, where will you find room for her to
    sleep?
How can your love for each other be revealed if she is
    left shivering in the cold?

If your heart loves her, and hers loves you,

Then, last evening in the courtyard where the swing is,
> when the night was far advanced,
And the flowers and the moon were hidden in darkness,
Had you, as you ought to have, availed yourself of that
> priceless time to show your love,
What need would there have been for addressing a poem
> to an expert poet?

I have pillows embroidered with birds of love,
And a silk coverlet of turquoise blue,
Which would captivate any heart;
But how could I lend them to you?
If you do not take off your clothes, what would it
> matter?
Would this not be better than if she does not come at all?
If your love is fulfilled, great indeed will be your
> blessing.'

She says:

> Mr. Chang, I wish to ask you frankly what your
> idea now is regarding my Young Mistress.

She sings:

'Her eyebrows are like the dark outline of the distant
> hills;
Her eyes are as dark as the pure water of autumn;
Her skin is milk-white;
Her waist is as pliant as the young willow;
Beautiful are her features, tender is her heart;
Kind and gentle are her manners and sedate is her
> nature.
She has no need to use magical moxa or the divine
> needle to effect a cure,
For she herself, like the Goddess of Mercy, can relieve
> you from your distress!'

She says:

However this may be, I am still incredulous.

She sings:

'Let me repeat the verses at leisure while you ponder them again.'

MR. CHANG *says:*

Miss Hung Niang, the case of to-day cannot be compared with that of the past.

HUNG NIANG *says:*

Ah! sir, I do not agree.

She sings:

'Your past has gone for ever.
I only speak of the present!'

She says:

I do not believe that my Young Mistress will really come to-night.

She sings:

'Why should she come to-night at so late an hour?'

MR. CHANG *says:*

Miss Hung Niang, let me tell you that you need not trouble yourself as to whether your Young Mistress will or will not come. All I expect from you is to do your best for me.

HUNG NIANG *sings:*

'I have never done anything else but my best for you,
Not in the hope of flawless jade or yellow gold as a reward;
All I want is to have my head covered with flowers and an embroidered gown reaching to the ground.

Even should the Mistress shut tight the door,

Sooner or later I will enable you to fulfil your heart's
    desire.'

She says:

Now, sir, may I also tell you that all I expect from
    you is that you will do your best for yourself, and
    I will not trouble myself as to whether my Young
    Mistress will or will not come.

She sings:

'When she comes, how can consent or refusal rest with
    her?
When you meet her, success or failure depends on you!'
[Exeunt.

PART IV

THE TITLES OF THE FOUR ACTS OF THE FOURTH PART

HUNG NIANG succeeds in making a happy union.

MADAM demands full details.

YING-YING drinks the stirrup-cup at the Pavilion of Farewell.

MR. CHANG dreams of YING-YING at the Bridge Inn.

ACT I

FULFILMENT OF THE BILLET-DOUX

YING-YING *enters, and says:*

> Hung Niang has gone with my missive, making an assignation with Mr. Chang to-night. I must await her return and decide how to act.

HUNG NIANG *enters, and says:*

> My Young Mistress ordered me to take a missive to Mr. Chang, making an assignation with him to-night. But being afraid that she would change her mind and drive him to destruction, which would be no trifle, I must go and see my Young Mistress and hear what she has to say.

YING-YING *says:*

> Hung Niang, get my bed ready. I am going to sleep.

HUNG NIANG *says:*

> It is all right about your going to sleep, but what is to be done with the man?

YING-YING *says:*

> What man?

HUNG NIANG *says:*

> My Young Mistress! There you are again. If you drive him to destruction, it would be no trifle! If you go back on your promise, I will inform my Mistress that you told me to take the missive making an assignation with Mr. Chang.

YING-YING *says:*

> You little cat, how artful you are!

HUNG NIANG *says:*

> It is not I who am artful but it is you who must not play the same trick again.

YING-YING *says:*

> But the very idea of this overwhelms me with bashfulness!

HUNG NIANG *says:*

> But who will see you? There is no one else except myself.

HUNG NIANG, *urging her, says:*

> Let us be off! Let us be off!
>
> > (YING-YING *maintains silence.*)

HUNG NIANG, *urging her, says:*

> My Young Mistress, there is nothing for it but for us to be off at once.
>
> > (YING-YING *maintains silence and reveals her feelings in dumb show.*)

HUNG NIANG, *urging her, says:*

> My Young Mistress, let us be off! Let us be off!
>
> > (YING-YING *maintains silence; proceeds, and then stands still.*)

HUNG NIANG, *urging her, says:*

> My Young Mistress, why do you stand still? Let us be off! Let us be off!
>
> > (YING-YING *maintains silence and proceeds.*)

HUNG NIANG *says:*

> Although my Young Mistress is determined in her speech, her steps have already yielded.

She sings:

'As my Young Mistress is pure in spirit and as beautiful
   as the flowers,
Her lover thinks of her incessantly from morn till eve!
To-night she has made a firm and sincere resolve
Which will cancel all the false promises I have made
Leaving her boudoir, she proceeds to the library,
While he, like the Prince of Ch'u, who left his country
   to meet the Fairy of Love,
Is using the arts of old to become united with her whom
   he loves.
My Young Mistress is like the Fairy of Love, and
   Mr. Chang is like the Prince of Ch'u.
The Prince of Ch'u is sure to be in readiness to meet
   his loved one at the trysting-place.'   [*Exeunt.*

MR. CHANG *enters, and says:*

The Young Lady ordered Hung Niang to bring a
missive, making an assignation with me to-night.
But the first watch of the night is already passed.
Why has she not come?

'This beautiful night on Earth is wrapped in silence,
But will the Fair One from Heaven ever come?'

He sings:

'I stand on the silent steps.
The night is far advanced and a fragrant vapour is
   spread throughout this golden space.
Solitary is the library,
And sad unto death is the student.

Where are the clouds with their varied colours which
   will bring me good news?

'AS THE SHADOWS OF THE FLOWERS MOVE IN THE MOONLIGHT,

'I THINK IT IS THE FAIR LADY APPROACHING'

The light of the moon, like a flood, covers the pavilion
and the terraces.
The priests repose in their cells.
The crows cry in the trees of the courtyard.
The sound of the wind in the bamboos
Makes me think that it is the jingling of her gold
ornaments.
As the shadows of the flowers move in the moonlight,
I think it is the Fair Lady approaching.
My mind is in suspense, my gaze is fixed,
And my loving heart is full of agitation.
I can find no repose either for body or mind.
In this time of stress I lean on the door, waiting.
But not a word of news arrives either by the Blue
Phoenix or the Yellow Dog.

With confused love thoughts of her, I am so wearied
that I can no longer keep my eyes open.
On my lonely pillow, I dreamt that I had almost reached
the trysting-place.
Had I foreseen that I should be tormented night and
day by thoughts of her,
I think it would have been much better had I never
met the beauty who could overthrow cities.
When one has made a mistake, he should blame himself
and be not afraid to correct it.
Even if I were prepared to withdraw my mind from
the love of beauty and apply it as sincerely to the
love of the virtuous, and to reform my heart,
How could I prevent her from possessing it?

I still lean on the door, resting my cheek on my hand,
How can I possibly guess whether she will come or not?

It may be that she will certainly find it difficult to leave
the side of her mother.
My eyes seem to burst with looking for her,
My heart to quail with thoughts of her.
Probably she, who is making me her victim, is herself
not at ease.'

He says:

She has not yet come. Is she not proving false
again?

He sings:

'If she is willing to come, she will have already left her
noble home;
And should she arrive she will fill my humble library
with happiness.
But if she does not come, my hopes will be gone like
a stone sunk in the vast ocean!
Counting my footsteps, I pace to and fro,
And then lean against the window-sill,
To send word to her so talented:

Although you have rebuffed me so cruelly,
I have never borne you malice in my heart,
So as to effect a change of mind and heart in you,
And to make you promise me to come at night and
stay till morning,
We have exchanged love glances for half a year,
During which period my feelings have been beyond
endurance.

I am ready to suffer wrong and prepared to be tricked.
I reflect that I, a stranger in a strange land, try to
force myself just to eat and drink enough to keep
myself alive,

All for the sake of you, whom I love to distraction!
I have steeled my heart to patient endurance.
It is only by my resolution and sincerity that I have
  been able to preserve my body from death.
Were an astrologer to be consulted about my six months
  of grief,
He would certainly say that it will require more than
  ten years for me to recover.'

HUNG NIANG *enters, and says:*

My Young Mistress, I will go ahead while you
wait here.

  (*She knocks at the door.*)

MR. CHANG *says:*

The Young Lady has arrived.

HUNG NIANG *says:*

My Young Mistress has arrived. You take her
coverlet and pillow.

MR. CHANG, *bowing, says:*

Miss Hung Niang, at this moment, words fail to
express my feelings. Only Heaven could reveal
them.

HUNG NIANG *says:*

Not so loud or you will frighten her. You stay
here and I will bring her in.

HUNG NIANG, *pushing* YING-YING *forward, says:*

My Young Mistress, you go in, and I will await
you outside the window.   [*Exit.*

MR. CHANG, *when he sees* YING-YING, *kneels and embraces
her, saying:*

How fortunate I am to have been able to trouble
you to come here, my Young Lady!

He sings:

> 'The sudden appearance of her whom I love to dis-
>   traction
> Has already almost entirely cured my sickness!
> Who could have hoped that you, who formerly rebuffed
>   me, would to-night treat me so cordially?
> As you, my Young Lady, have shown such affection,
> It is only right that your stupid admirer, Chang Kung,
>   should salute you on his knees.
> I have neither the grace of Sung Yü,
> Nor the good looks of P'an An,
> Nor the talents of Tzu-chien.
> Fair Lady! you must take pity on me, a stranger in a
>   strange land.'

        (YING-YING *maintains silence.*)

        (MR. CHANG *rises and sits close to* YING-YING.)

He sings:

> 'Her embroidered shoes are only half a span long;
> Her willowy waist, one hand could enfold.
> Overwhelmed with bashfulness, she refuses to raise her
>   head,
> And rest it on the pillow embroidered with love-birds.
> Her golden hair-pins seem to be falling from her locks.
> The more disarranged her hair becomes, the more
>   beautiful she appears!
> I will unbutton your robe and untie your silk girdle.
> A fragrance like that of the lily and musk permeates
>   the solitary library.
> You wicked one! Well do you know how to enslave me!
> Oh! why do you not turn your face to me?'

        (MR. CHANG *embraces* YING-YING.)

        (YING-YING *remains silent.*)

He sings:

    'I clasp to my breast her who is like jade, but softer,
        and who is fragrant and warm.
    Ah! At last, like Liu and Yüan, I am in paradise.
    The spring is here and the flowers are in bloom.
    Her waist is like a willow in its pliancy.
    The heart of the flower has been gently plucked,
    And the drops of dew make the peony open.

    Overwhelmed with joy,
    I am as happy as a fish delighting in water.
    And, like a butterfly, which keeps gathering the sweet
        fragrance from the delicate buds.
    You half reject me and half welcome me,
    While I am filled with surprise and love!
    With my fragrant mouth I kiss your sweet cheeks.

    The pure, white silk handkerchief
    Is stained with spots of delicate red.
    As I take a furtive glance at her under the light of the
        lamp,
    I see her lovely, swelling breast.
    And to my great surprise and wonder,
    So exquisite and pure is her full figure,
    That I do not know where her loveliness begins!
    Poor student Chang, a lonely traveller from the West
        of Lo-yang!
    Ever since he met her, he has never been able to forget
        her.
    He was consumed in sorrow because of the separation,
    And had no means to cure his love-sickness!
    Now thanks to this charming girl, who has pardoned
        his rudeness, the romance is fulfilled.

I love you with all my heart and soul.
I have defiled your virgin purity.
I had forgotten my meals and abandoned my sleep, and
    was prepared for the worst.
If I had not borne all this with sincerity and patience,
How could I have been able to end the bitterness of
    love with perfect bliss!

To-night I have completed my happiness.
My soul seems to have flown to the highest heavens.
I have at last met you, my Young Lady, so full of love.
Behold! how my figure has wasted and how my body
    has become as thin as a stalk!
The happy union of to-night still seems to me unreal.
But the dew is falling on the fragrant earth,
The breeze is blowing gently over the lonely steps,
The moonlight is shining on the library,
And the clouds are enveloping the trysting-place.
Observing clearly these surroundings,
How can I say that our meeting is only a dream?'

MR. CHANG *rises, kneels, thanks her, and says:*
    I, Chang Kúng, having been able to wait upon you
    to-night, will be for ever grateful to you.

      (YING-YING *maintains silence.*)

HUNG NIANG *enters, and, prompting* YING-YING, *says:*
    My Young Mistress, you had better return, in
    case the Mistress may discover our absence.

      (YING-YING *arises, starts to go, and maintains
      silence.*)

      (MR. CHANG, *holding* YING-YING'S *hand, keeps
      gazing at her.*)

He sings:

'Sadness seems inevitable!

How full of charm, how perfect in beauty she is!
At first sight she makes one love her;
When not seen for a moment, she fills one with regret;
And the sight of her, even for a short time, inspires
affection!
To-night we have met within the blue gauze curtains,
But when shall I again untie the fragrant silk girdle?'

HUNG NIANG, *urging her, says:*

My Young Mistress, let us return quickly, in case
the Mistress may discover our absence.

(YING-YING, *remaining silent, descends the
steps.*)

(MR. CHANG, *holding both* YING-YING'S *hands,
keeps gazing at her.*)

MR. CHANG *sings:*

'The feelings of love have permeated her snow-white
bosom,
The expression of love is revealed through her black
eyebrows,
Making the most precious things poor in comparison
with her attractive. beauty.
Her face, like an apricot, and her cheeks, like peaches,
In the bright moonlight
Show more clearly the beautiful contrast of red and
white.
In descending the fragrant steps,
She treads the green moss with hesitation,
Not on account of her shoes, embroidered with the
phoenix, being too small.

176

I regret that the poor scholar is unworthy of your
    love;
I thank you, who are full of charm, for the love you
    have mistakenly bestowed on me,
And hope that you will try to find time to come again
    earlier than to-night!'   [*Exeunt*.

ACT II

HUNG NIANG IN THE DOCK

MADAM *enters with her adopted son,* HUAN LANG, *and says:*

> During the last few days I have noticed that Ying-ying is confused in her speech, most unusually wrapped in thought; that her figure and her manner are not the same as formerly; and this makes me feel very uneasy.

HUAN LANG *says:*

> The other night, when you were asleep, I saw the Young Lady and Hung Niang go to the garden to burn incense. Though I waited half the night, they had not come back.

MADAM *says:*

> Go and tell Hung Niang to come here.
>
> (HUAN LANG *calls* HUNG NIANG.)

HUNG NIANG *enters, and says:*

> My Young Master, what have you called me for?

HUAN LANG *says:*

> The Mistress has learned that you and the Young Mistress have been to the garden. Now she wants to question you.

HUNG NIANG, *alarmed, says:*

> Alas! My Young Mistress, you have compromised me! My Young Master, you go ahead and I will come directly.

178

'The precious pond is full of water, on which the love-
   birds sleep.
The wind has blown open the embroidered curtain of
   the door and the parrot has learned the secret.'

She sings:

'Had you but gone by night and returned at dawn
Your joys could have lasted as long as Heaven and
   Earth endure.
It is only because you wished to meet in happy union,
You always made me as anxious as if my heart were in
   my mouth.
You ought to have gone at moonlight and returned
   with the morning stars.
Who would ever have allowed you to sleep there all
   night long?
The Mistress is of a very ingenious mind and staid
   nature;
And furthermore, by plausible words and specious
   arguments, can make something out of nothing.

She must have suspected that this poor wretch of a
   Scholar has made himself her son-in-law.
That you, my Young Mistress, have become his sweet
   wife.
And that I, the maid Hung Niang, have pulled the
   strings.
Furthermore, not to speak of the beauty of your clearly
   marked eyebrows, and the sparkling of your bright
   eyes,
If you only try your girdle and the buttons of your
   robe,
And compare it with the size of your former figure,

You will find that you have a vitality and grace quite different from before!'

She says:

I feel sure when I have to appear before my Mistress she will say: 'Oh, you little wretch!'

She sings:

'I ordered you to go with the sole object of watching her at every turn;

What on earth made you lead her astray into such bad ways?

Should she thus address me, what have I to say in my defence?'

She says:

Then I will simply say to her: 'I, your maid Hung Niang, ever since my childhood, have never dared to deceive you, my Mistress.'

She sings:

'And then I will make a clean breast of the whole affair!'

She says:

What had I to gain from their liaison?

She sings:

'Their heads were as close together as two lilies on one stem,

Like two love-birds, they indulged their affection to the full,

While I, remaining outside the window alone, never dared to cough even slightly,

And stood on the damp moss until my embroidered shoes were frozen like ice.

Now my delicate skin is about to receive the impact of
a thick rod.

What profit have I, the go-between of these two lovers,
derived?'

She says:

Well, my Young Mistress, I am off! If I can
explain matters to her satisfaction, don't you be
too joyful; and if I fail, don't be too down-
hearted! You remain here and await the news.

HUNG NIANG *appears before* MADAM, *who says:*

You little wretch! Why don't you kneel down at
once? Do you confess your guilt?

HUNG NIANG *says:*

Your maid, Hung Niang, has no guilt to confess!

MADAM *says:*

Do you still insist on denying it with your lips?
If you tell the truth I will pardon you. If you do
not I will beat you to death, you little wretch!
You, with the Young Lady, went at midnight to
the garden.

HUNG NIANG *says:*

Never! Who saw us?

MADAM *says:*

My son, Huan Lang, saw you, and you still deny it?

(*She beats her.*)

HUNG NIANG *says:*

My Mistress, withdraw your noble hand! I beseech you to calm your wrath while you listen to
what your maid, Hung Niang, has to say.

She sings:

'When we were sitting at night, having finished our
   sewing and embroidery,
I chatted with my Young Mistress about nothing in
   particular.
It was mentioned that elder brother (Mr. Chang) had
   been sick for long,
So it was decided that we two, unknown to Madam,
   should go to the library to inquire after him.'

MADAM *says:*

To inquire?   What did he say?

HUNG NIANG *sings:*

'He said that recently the Mistress had returned evil
   for good,
And had suddenly caused his joy to be turned to sadness.
He said: "Hung Niang, you go back first!"
He said further: "The Young Mistress will remain
   behind temporarily." '

MADAM *says:*

Ai! Yah! You wretch! She, an unmarried girl,
to be left behind?

HUNG NIANG *sings:*

'Of course! To enable him to be treated by the ever-
   healing needle and the moxa cure.
But who would have thought it could end in the case
   of the swallows mating and the orioles pairing!
The young couple have continued to keep each other
   company for more than a month.
What necessity is there to go into minute detail?
They both know not grief nor sorrow,
Being devoted to each other in heart and soul!

My Mistress, do overlook the matter if you can!
Why should you probe into it too deeply?'

MADAM *says:*

> It is you, you little wretch, who are the cause of
> all this trouble.

HUNG NIANG *says:*

> This trouble has nothing to do with Mr. Chang,
> my Young Mistress, or your maid, Hung Niang,
> but is entirely your fault, my Mistress!

MADAM *says:*

> You little wretch, you are unjustly implicating me!
> How is it my fault?

HUNG NIANG *says:*

> Good faith is the base of human dealings. With-
> out such good faith one is not worthy of the name
> of man. When P'u Chiu Monastery was sur-
> rounded by the army of bandits you promised to
> give your daughter as wife to him who made the
> bandits retire. If Mr. Chang had not been the
> devoted admirer of the beauty of my Young Mis-
> tress, why should he, who had nothing to do with
> the matter, have contrived such a good plan?
> You, my Mistress, after the bandits had retreated
> and you were left in peace, repented and went back
> on your former promise. Was not this a breach
> of good faith? Being unwilling to consent to the
> match, you ought to have rewarded him with
> money and made him go away far from here. It
> was very wrong of you to keep him in the library,
> immediately adjoining the Young Lady's abode,
> thereby enabling the pining maid and the lonely
> bachelor to peep at each other, which has thus
> resulted in this trouble. If you, my Mistress, do
> not cover up this scandal, in the first place, the

183

family records of the Prime Minister will be overwhelmed with disgrace; in the second place, Mr.
Chang, who has been our benefactor, will be unjustly insulted by us; and in the third place, if the
matter is taken up officially, you, my Mistress,
will be the first to suffer for the offence of not
having looked after your family properly. According to Hung Niang's humble opinion, nothing is
better than to forgive small offences as so to carry
out to completion a great event. Such a course
would certainly be of great advantage in the
present case.

She sings:

'The proverb says: When a girl is grown up, it is no
good to keep her at home.

One is a leading literary luminary,
And the other is the foremost lady scholar;
One is thoroughly versed in the three religions and the
nine schools,
And the other is an expert in drawing and embroidering
the phoenix.
When there is such a romance as this, which is not
unusual in this world, it is best to let it take its
course and not to interfere with it.
How can you make an enemy of a great benefactor,
Who summoned his old friend, the General of the
White Horse,
Who came and beheaded the miserable bandit, the
Flying Tiger?
Putting aside the impossibility of keeping Mr. Chang,
the Scholar, apart from his beloved, and merely
regarding them as if they were two stars arising at
different times,

There is still to be considered what a disgrace and
dishonour it would be to the family of the Prime
Minister, Ts'ui, if the matter became known!

And as this is, after all, a case which concerns one of
your own flesh and blood,

You, my Mistress, should not probe into it farther.'

MADAM *says*:

> After all, what the little wretch has said is quite
> reasonable. It is my misfortune that I am the
> mother of such an unworthy girl. If the case is
> brought before the authorities it will certainly
> overwhelm our family with disgrace. Well! Well!
> My family has never had any male guilty of any
> offence against the law or any female who has
> married a second time. So I must give my
> daughter to this beast. Hung Niang, first go and
> tell that bad girl to come here.

HUNG NIANG *calls her* YOUNG MISTRESS, *and says*:

> My Young Mistress, the rod was brandished over
> the whole of my body without cessation. But, by
> speaking out straight, I was spared. Now my
> Mistress asks you to go to see her.

YING-YING *says*:

> How can I go to see my mother when I am over-
> whelmed with shame?

HUNG NIANG *says*:

> Ah, my Young Mistress, you are at it again! Why
> should you feel ashamed in the presence of your
> mother? If you feel ashamed you should not have
> acted as you did!

She sings:

'When the bright moon had just risen over the top of
the willows,

You had already fulfilled your assignation with your
lover in the dusk.

This made me feel so ashamed that I turned my face
away and bit into the sleeves of my robe with my
teeth.

How could I dare to fix my gaze on you?

All that I saw was the delicate points of the soles of
your shoes.

One abandoned himself to love with ardour unceasing,

While the other doted on him in silence.

At that time you did not show the slightest sign of
shame.'

YING-YING *meets her* MOTHER, *who says:*

My dear child!

(MADAM *weeps.*)

(YING-YING *weeps.*)

(HUNG NIANG *weeps.*)

MADAM *says:*

My dear child, you have been imposed upon and
wronged. The act you have committed is entirely
due to my sins in a former existence. How can I
blame anybody else? Should I report the matter
officially it would be an overwhelming disgrace to
your father. Such an act is not one of which a
Prime Minister's family like ours would be guilty.

(YING-YING *weeps very bitterly.*)

MADAM *says:*

Hung Niang, help your Young Mistress. Well!

Well! The whole trouble is due to my daughter not having proved herself worthy. Go to the library and tell that beast to come.

(HUNG NIANG *calls* MR. CHANG.)

MR. CHANG *says:*

Who is calling me?

HUNG NIANG *says:*

Your affair has been discovered. My Mistress is calling for you.

MR. CHANG *says:*

There seems to be no way out of the difficulty but for you to screen me a little. I wonder who told Madam this! I am trembling with fear. How can I go to see her?

HUNG NIANG *says:*

Don't appear to be afraid but put on a bold air and go at once to see her.

She sings:

'The truth having leaked out, the matter could not stop there,

So I had to confess at once.

She has now prepared tea and wine to entertain you,

Reversing the usual custom of the man having to make the first approach,

And you are full of anxiety instead of being pleased.

What need is there of a betrothal arranged by a go-between,

Though I have not discharged thoroughly my duty as chaperon?

187

You are really as useless as a stalk of grain that bears
no ears,
And as a spear-head that looks like silver but is really
wax!'

(MR. CHANG *meets* MADAM.)

MADAM *says:*

You are a fine scholar, indeed! Have you not
heard that conduct unworthy of the ancient sages
should never be indulged in? Should I hand you
over to the authorities, that would only over-
whelm my family with disgrace. There is therefore nothing left for me but to take my daughter,
Ying-ying, and marry her to you as your wife.
But for three generations past our family has never
had a son-in-law who had no official rank. So you
must proceed to the Capital to-morrow to attend
the highest examination. In the meantime I will
take care of your future wife. If you succeed in
getting office you may come to see me; but if you
fail do not come.

(MR. CHANG, *maintaining silence, kneels and
makes his bows.*)

HUNG NIANG *says:*

Thank Heaven, thank Earth, and thanks to my
Mistress!

She sings:

'Your love-affair having been entirely forgiven,
You can forthwith raise your eyebrows which were
formerly knitted;
And now will really commence the enjoyment of your
devoted love in peace.

Who would hope for such bliss?
The beauty of such a delightful maiden can only be
    enjoyed by him who is worthy of it!'

MADAM *says:*

    Hung Niang, you give orders for the luggage to
be packed, and prepare the wine, viands, and
sweetmeats, so that to-morrow, when we escort
Mr. Chang to the Pavilion of Farewell, we may
give him a farewell feast.

'Send word to the willows that grow by the bank of the
    West river,
To look kindly on the traveller who is about to depart.'

                    [*Exit* MADAM *with* YING-YING.

HUNG NIANG *says:*

    Mr. Chang, do you feel happy or sad?

She sings:

'We must just wait till you come back again,
When flutes and drums will sound at that joyful time
    throughout the painted hall,
And when you two love-birds are joined in matrimony,
Then, and only then, I will receive from you a reward
    for my acting as go-between,
And drink a cup of wine offered by you in appreciation
    of my services.'   [*Exeunt.*

ACT III

A FEAST WITH TEARS

MADAM *enters, and says:*

>To-day we are going to see Mr. Chang start for the Capital, so, Hung Niang, go at once and tell your Young Mistress that she must come with us to the Pavilion of Farewell. I have already given orders for a feast to be prepared, and have also sent an invitation to Mr. Chang. I feel sure that he must have finished his packing by this time.

YING-YING, *with* HUNG NIANG, *enters, and says:*

>To-day, we are going to see him off. To say good-bye at any time is very sad, but how much more painful is it when the time is late autumn!

MR. CHANG *enters, and says:*

>Last night Madam said I must go to the Capital to attend the highest examination, and if I return, having obtained office, she will then give me her daughter in marriage. There is nothing for it but for me to go, as she directed. I now start first for the Pavilion of Farewell to wait there for the Young Lady so that I may bid her farewell.

>>*[Exit.*

YING-YING *says:*

>'Whether there be joy at meeting or sorrow at parting, a glass of wine is drunk;
>To the four corners of the world, man, mounted on his horse, is always on the move.'

She sings:

> 'Grey are the clouds in the sky and faded are the leaves
> on the ground,
> Bitter is the west wind as the wild geese fly from the
> north to the south.
> How is it that in the morning the white-frosted trees
> are dyed as red as a wine-flushed face?
> It must have been caused by the tears of those who are
> about to be separated.

> My regret is that we met so late,
> And my sorrow is that we have to part so soon,
> Long though the willow branches may be, it is im-
> possible to tie to them the white steed in order to
> delay his departure.
> I pray you, O autumn forest, to hinder the setting of
> the sun for my sake.
> May his steed go slowly,
> And may my carriage follow it without delay.
> Just as we had declared our love openly for each other,
> The first thing to happen to us is that we are to be
> separated.
> When suddenly I heard a voice say "I am going",
> The shock made my golden bracelets too large for me!
> When I saw in the distance the Pavilion of Farewell,
> My body seemed to waste away.'

HUNG NIANG *says:*

> My Young Mistress, you have not made your
> toilet to-day!

YING-YING *says:*

> Hung Niang, how can you know the feelings of my
> heart?

She sings:

'Who can understand this sorrow of mine?

When I have seen the carriage and horse ready to start,
How can I fail to feel full of anguish and sorrow?
And how can I have the heart to make myself look
    beautiful and charming?
All I want is to prepare my coverlet and my pillow
And have a sound sleep.
Who cares that my robe and its sleeves are wet through
    with my never-ceasing tears?
Oh! how sorrowful unto death am I!
Yea unto death!
Later on I will write to him and give him tidings,
Sad and lonely though I may feel!'

> (MADAM, YING-YING, *and* HUNG NIANG *arrive
> at the Pavilion of Farewell.*)

> (MR. CHANG *profoundly salutes* MADAM.)

> (YING-YING *turns her face away.*)

MADAM *says:*

Mr. Chang, come nearer. Now that you are my
own flesh and blood, it is not necessary for you and
my daughter to avoid each other. My child, you
come here to meet him.

> (MR. CHANG *and* YING-YING *meet each other.*)

MADAM *says:*

Mr. Chang, you sit down there. I will sit here,
and my child there. Hung Niang, pour out the
wine. Mr. Chang, you drink this cup and leave
no heel-tap. Since I have promised to marry my
daughter to you, you must go to the Capital and

prove yourself worthy of my child. You must make every effort to come out first on the list at the highest examination.

Mr. CHANG *says:*

I, Chang Kung, am a man of poor talents and shallow learning, but depending entirely on the favour and deserved good fortune of the late Prime Minister, and of you, Madam, whatever happens, I must come back with my name first on the list, so that the Young Lady may in due course be ennobled!

(*They all sit down.*)

(YING-YING *sighs.*)

YING-YING *sings:*

'The west wind blows and the faded leaves are scattered everywhere.

Covered by the cold mist, the decayed grass presents a sorry sight.

He sits uneasily at the feast,

And I see him knitting his eyebrows in sorrow as if he is about to die.

I dare not let the tears which fill my eyes fall,

Lest others should know my sorrow.

When I am suddenly seen by others, I lower my head,

And, sighing deeply, I pretend to arrange my white silk robe.

Although in future ours will be a happy union,

How can I at this moment refrain from sorrow and weeping?

I am so mad and intoxicated with love,

That since last night

My slight figure has become to-day still slighter.

Before the joy of our happy union had been completed
The sorrow of departure arrived.
Formerly we loved each other in secret,
Last night our love was clearly revealed,
But to-day we have to separate!
Though I have just realized the bitterness of those days
    when we suffered from love-sickness,
Who would have thought that the sorrow of separation
    is ten times worse?'

MADAM *says:*

    Hung Niang, help your Young Mistress to pour
    out the wine.

        (YING-YING *pours out the wine.*)

        (MR. CHANG *sighs.*)

YING-YING *whispers to him:*

    You drink this cup of wine as I hold it in my hand.

She sings:

'You are abandoning me, treating lightly a long farewell
As if entirely oblivious of our happy union
When your cheeks rested on mine,
And when we held each other by the hand.
To be the son-in-law of the Prime Minister Ts'ui
Will ennoble you as being the husband of a wife of a
    distinguished family.
Is not such a happy match, like two lotuses on one stem,
Better than the attainment of the highest literary
    honours?'

        (YING-YING *sits down at the table again, and
          sighs.*)

She sings:

'The feast is passing too quickly.

194

This moment we are together
But in another moment we shall be separated.
Were it not for the presence of my mother at the feast,
    which necessitates my acting with usual propriety,
I should like to show my respect for him by raising the
    dish for him to the level of my eyebrows.
Although this joyous meeting is but for a moment,
We, as husband and wife, should have enjoyed it sitting
    at the same table.
I have tried in vain to show my devotion to him with
    my eyes,
And as I kept thinking over the whole matter
I was almost petrified into stone like the wife who
    longed for the return of her husband.'

MADAM *says:*

Hung Niang, pour out the wine.

After having poured out a cup for MR. CHANG, HUNG
    NIANG *pours out a cup for* YING-YING, *and says:*

My Young Mistress, you have not had breakfast
this morning, so will you please drink a little?

YING-YING *sings:*

'The wine and food you have offered to me
Taste like earth and mud,
But even if they were earth and mud,
They would have some of the aroma of earth and the
    flavour of mud.

This warmed wine of highest quality
Seems to me as tasteless and cold as water,
And the cup appears to be more than half full of tears
    of love.
The tea and rice before me remain untasted,

Because I am filled with regrets and sorrow.
It is only for empty fame, as unimportant as a snail's
    horn,
And for trifling profit, as large as a fly's head,
That the two love-birds are torn apart and made to stay
    in different places,
One in one place, and one in another,
Heaving deep sighs for each other.

In a moment cups and dishes will be removed,
And the carriage will go east and the horse west;
Both lingering on their way
As the sun sets behind the green hills.
How can I know where he will dwell to-night?
Even in my dreams it will be impossible to find him.'

MADAM *says:*

> Hung Niang, order them to get ready the carriage
> and request Mr. Chang to mount his pony. I am
> going to return with your Young Mistress.

> (*They all get ready to start.*)

> (MR. CHANG *makes his bow to* MADAM.)

MADAM *says:*

> I have nothing else to say to you except that I hope
> you will keep in mind the desirability of securing
> high rank, and come back soon.

MR. CHANG, *thanking her, says:*

> I will be careful to obey your strict instructions.

> (MR. CHANG *and* YING-YING *bow to each other.*)

YING-YING *says:*

> Now you are going, whether you secure official
> rank or not see that you come back again as quickly
> as possible.

MR. CHANG *says:*

> My Young Lady, make yourself easy on that score. If the highest literary rank is not to be gained by your family, what other family can gain it? I must now bid you farewell.

YING-YING *says:*

> Wait a moment. I have no other farewell gift to present to you except an impromptu short poem.

'Deserted and abandoned, what can I say now—
I, whom once you loved so fondly?
But may your devotions of old
Be bestowed on her whom you love next.'

MR. CHANG *says:*

> My Young Lady, you quite mistake me! How could I ever think of loving any one else but you? As to this poem, my heart at this moment is in a state of confusion. My Young Lady will not believe what I might say, so I must wait until I have returned, after having attained the highest literary honours, when I will respond to your poem with one of mine.

YING-YING *sings:*

'My red sleeves are soaked with my tears of love,
But well I know that your blue gown is more soaked
    still.
The oriole flies to the east and the swallow to the west.
Even before he starts I ask the date of his return.
Although he, who is now before my eyes, is about to
    go afar,
I will, for the present, drink a cup of wine in his honour.

Before I have even tasted it, my heart is intoxicated.
My eyes shed tears of blood,
My feelings of love are turned to ashes.

When you arrive at the Capital,
May the climate agree with you.
As you pursue your route
Be moderate in what you drink and eat,
Take care of your all-precious health at every season.
In the deserted villages, at the time of rain and dew,
    you should seek sleep early;
In the country inn, when there is wind and frost, you
    should rise late.
When riding in the chilly autumn wind,
With no one to look after you,
You yourself should pay every attention to your well-
    being.

To whom can I tell my cares and sorrows?
It is only I, myself, who know the pains of love.
Even Heaven cares nothing for human sufferings.
My tears would more than fill the winding waters of
    the Yellow River,
And the load of my grief would weigh down the three
    peaks of the Hua Mountain.
When night falls in the upper story of the Western
    Chamber,
I will watch the evening sun falling on the old road,
And the withered willows by the long embankment.

Not long ago we came together from one place,
And now we are departing each on a separate way.
When I reach home, I shall dread to look inside the
    silken curtains of my couch.

Last night the embroidered coverlet was unusually
  warm where love still dwelt;
To-day the green counterpane will be cold, and he will
  be present to me only in my dreams.
I can devise no plans to detain him here.
He has mounted his steed,
While both of us have tears in our eyes and sorrow in
  our looks.

I am not anxious as to whether your good fortune will
  be as perfect as your learning,
But my sole anxiety is whether you will give up one
  wife for another!
The fish of the river and the wild goose in the sky will
  be the bearers of many letters from you.
While I here will frequently send you tidings by the
  Blue Phoenix.
Swear not that you will never come back unless your
  name is on the list of honours at the examinations!
But bear in mind that if elsewhere you see fair beauties,
You must not linger there as you have done here.'

MR. CHANG *says:*

My Young Lady, your words, as precious to me
as gold and jade, are imprinted on my heart. We
will meet again soon, so you need not be too sad.
I am now going.

'I restrain my tears, and try to conceal them by hanging
  down my head;
Though overwhelmed by my feelings, I assume a look
  of delight.'

YING-YING *says:*

'My soul has already gone from me,

199

傷離

'MY SOUL HAS ALREADY GONE FROM ME,

HOW CAN I FOLLOW YOU EVEN IN MY DREAMS?'

How can I follow you even in my dreams?

                     [*Exit* Mr. CHANG.

    (YING-YING *sighs*.)

She sings:

> 'The green mountain that separates us prevents me
>   from seeing him off,
> The thin-planted wood seems to bear me a grudge by
>   obscuring him from my sight.
> The slight mist and the night vapours screen him from
>   view.
> The evening sun falls on the old road and no human
>   voice is heard,
> But only the rustling of the crops in the autumn wind
>   and the neigh of the horse.
> Reluctantly I mount my carriage.
> How very hurriedly I came,
> But how slowly I return!'

MADAM *says:*

> Hung Niang, help your Young Mistress to mount
> her carriage. The time is already late; let us return
> at once.

> 'Though I have indirectly appeared to give way to my
>   dear daughter,
> I may be considered, after all, to have acted as a correct
>   and stern mother!'   [*Exit.*

HUNG NIANG *says:*

> The chariot with your mother is already a long
> way ahead, so, my Young Mistress, you must
> quickly return.

YING-YING *says:*

> Hung Niang, where do you think he has reached?

202

She sings:

'He is now in the midst of the mountains,
And his whip can be seen in the dying rays of the sun.
All the sorrows of the world seem to be accumulated
    in my breast.
How can a carriage of this size bear such a burden?'
                         [*Exeunt.*

ACT IV

A SURPRISING DREAM

Mr. Chang, *with his* Lute-bearer, *enters and says:*

We are already thirty miles east of P'u, and there,
before us, is the Bridge Inn. I will pass the night
there and go on to-morrow early. My horse is
unwilling to go farther at any price.

He sings:

'I see the lonely monastery at the east of P'u, hidden
by the evening clouds.

The melancholy arising from the faded leaves, of which
half the forest has been denuded, is the same as
the feelings caused by my separation.

When the horse moves slowly the rider is listless;

When the wind is strong the row of wild geese is
broken.

My regrets become all the more intense because this is
the very first night of our separation!

Last night our green coverlet was full of the fragrance
of lily and musk,

As we reclined on our pillows with our cheeks together.

Gazing intently upon her, I loved her to distraction.

Her locks were spread out like clouds, and in them was
inserted a comb of jade,

Which resembled the new moon half revealing itself.'

He says:

I have just arrived. Where is the Innkeeper?

The INNKEEPER *says:*

> Sir, this is the well-known Bridge Inn. The best
> room is at your disposal, sir.   [*Exit.*

MR. CHANG *says:*

> Lute-bearer, look after my horse, and have a lamp
> lit. I want nothing to eat. What I do want is a
> little sleep.

The LUTE BEARER *says:*

> Your servant is also very fatigued and badly in
> want of rest, so I will spread my bedding in front
> of your bed.

> (*The* LUTE-BEARER *falls asleep first.*)

MR. CHANG *says:*

> How can sleep visit my eyes to-night?

He sings:

> 'In the inn I recline on my lonely pillow.
> The sound of the autumn insect is heard on all sides.
> And to increase my sorrow,
> The wind cracks the paper windows.
> Sleeping alone for the first time
> I find the coverlet too thin and chilly.
> Lonely and cold, when shall I feel genial and warm
>   again?'

MR. CHANG *tries to sleep, but, tossing about, finds sleep a
stranger. He tries again and drops sound asleep.
Dreaming, he asks himself:*

> Is this the voice of my Young Lady? Where on
> earth am I now? I must get up and listen.

> (*Singing is heard.* MR. CHANG *listens.*)

205

'I SEE THE LONELY MONASTERY AT THE EAST

OF P'U, HIDDEN BY THE EVENING CLOUDS'

This is the song heard:

  'Walking in the lonely wilds and barren plains,
  I cannot restrain my girlish heart from fear.
  Panting along and gasping for breath,
  I struggle to overtake him as quickly as I can.'

MR. CHANG *says:*

    That is undoubtedly my Young Lady's voice, but
    whom is she trying to overtake?   I must listen again.

The song:

  'I beat the grass and startle the snakes.

  My heart feeling torn in two,
  I shrink not from this journey, long though it be,
  Keeping it secret from my mother
  And unknown to my waiting-maid.'

MR. CHANG *says:*

    It is quite clear that this is my Young Lady.   I will
    listen again.

The song:

  'When I saw him mounting his steed and heaving very
     sad sighs,
  It made me weep as if I were beside myself.
  It is not that I am infirm of mind,
  But even at the first setting of the sun after we had
     parted
  My sorrow was supreme,
  And I began to waste away.
  After even the lapse of half a day I had to tighten my
     skirt three or four folds.
  Who has ever before experienced such wearing away?'

Mr. Chang *says:*

What you say is true, my Young Lady. But where are you now?

> (*He listens again.*)

The song:

'Our short union had only just been happily completed
When, alas, ambition for office caused our separation.
The long suffering of our former sorrow had just been slightly relieved
When now we have to endure the never-ending thoughts arising out of our being parted from each other.'

Mr. Chang *says:*

The sentiments of my Young Lady's heart are evidently the same as mine. How very sad it is!

> (*He sighs, and listens again.*)

The song:

'The green grass is made to look pure by the bright frost;
The white dew covers all the faded leaves.
Up and down the road goes, uneven and winding.
The wind from all sides blows furiously.
While I am hurrying here,
Where are you resting now?'

Mr. Chang *says:*

My Young Lady, I am here. Come in.

He suddenly wakens, and says:

Ai-ya! Where am I? (*He looks and says:*) Pooh! After all, it's only the Bridge Inn.

> (*He calls for his* Lute-bearer, *who, being fast asleep, does not answer. He tries to go to*

sleep again, but fails and tosses about. He looks round again and is wrapped in thought.)

He sings:

'Dull indeed am I in this inn, with no one to speak to,
And so melancholy am I that this night seems like years.'

He says:

I have not the slightest idea what the time is now.

He sings:

'Is this evening, when the rain falls on the cold insects?
Or is it the morning, when the wind blows and the moon is about to disappear?
Where really am I, who have slept off my night's drinking?'

(*He falls asleep and dreams again.*)

YING-YING *enters, and, knocking at the door, says:*

Open the door! Open the door!

MR. CHANG *says:*

Who is knocking at the door? It is a female voice. How strange! I will not open the door.

He sings:

'If you are a human being, explain yourself at once;
If you are a ghost, vanish with all speed!'

YING-YING *says:*

It is I. Quickly open the door.

(MR. CHANG *opens the door, and leads* YING-YING *in by the hand.*)

MR. CHANG *sings:*

> 'Hearing that it is you, I at once take you by your
> fragrant silk sleeve.
> Ah!　So it is you!　My Young Lady!　My Young Lady!

YING-YING *says:*

> I thought to myself that as you have gone, how
> could I live without you?　So I have specially come
> to accompany you.

MR. CHANG *says:*

> It would be impossible to find another with a heart
> like yours.

He sings:

> 'You are thoroughly true to the last.
> With your raiment in disorder,
> And your embroidered shoes covered with dew and
> mud,
> The soles of your feet must be worn out by walking.
>
> At first you abandoned your sleep and forgot your food,
> To the injury of your fragrance and beauty;
> Your state being even worse than that of the flower that
> has faded after it has bloomed.
> When one's pillow is lonely and coverlet cold,
> When the male and female phoenix are separated,
> When a happy union is ended, like the full moon hidden
> in clouds,
> How could one but feel full of sadness?
>
> I think the saddest thing in life is separation.
> You have taken pity upon me travelling afar and alone
> over hill and dale.
> You have been worrying yourself to such distraction

That it would be best to break off our friendship and
our love.
But if our union is to terminate like a faded flower or
a half moon,
I am afraid it will be the case of a jar that has been crashed
or a jade hair ornament that has snapped in two.
It is not a lover heroic and powerful you desire,
Nor one who is proud and rich!
But all you do wish is that you and I, in life, should
share the same couch,
And in death the same grave!'

A SOLDIER *enters.* MR. CHANG *is startled. The* SOLDIER
says:

I just saw a young lady cross the river. I don't
know where she has gone. Light a torch. She
must have gone into this inn. Make her come out.
Make her come out!

MR. CHANG *says:*

What can be done? My Young Lady, you stand
behind me, and I will speak to him.

[*Exit* YING-YING.

MR. CHANG *sings:*

'You once violently attacked the P'u Chiu Monastery
with hoe and spade;
And now you are forcibly holding your sword and
battleaxe at my throat.
With the heart of a brigand and the mind of a robber,
you are the greatest rogue ever born!'

The SOLDIER *says:*

To what family does that young lady belong? How
dare you hide her?

Mr. Chang *sings:*

'Silence and avaunt!
Know you not what a courageous hero General Tu is?
With a mere glance he will make mincemeat of
  you,
And pointing his finger at you, he will make you a
  bloody mass;
And here he comes, riding his white charger!'

[*Exit the* Soldier, *in fear.*

Mr. Chang, *embracing his* Lute-bearer, *says:*
My Young Lady, you have been frightened.

The Lute-bearer *says:*
Sir, what do you mean?

(Mr. Chang *awakens, and reveals in dumb
  show his feelings.*)

Mr. Chang *says:*
Ah! After all it was but a dream. I will open the
door and look. All I see is the atmosphere is full
of the vapours of the dew, all the ground is covered
with hoar-frost, the morning star is just rising, and
the fading moon is still bright.

'The innocent twittering of the swallows and sparrows
  on the high branches
Prevents the fulfilment of the happy dream of the union
  of the love-birds!'

He sings:
'Green indeed are the willows which half conceal the
  high wall.
Profound is the silence of this beautiful autumn night
  outside the door.

213

Gentle is the breeze which makes the leaves fall from
the branches of the trees.

Melancholy are the rays of the moon in the clouds as
they pass through the window.

Tremulously, like the wriggling of dragons and snakes,
move the shadows of the bamboos.

I am transported into space like the Philosopher Chuang
when he dreamt that he was a butterfly.

Incessant is the chirping of the cricket.

Never-ending is the distant sound of the beating on
the washing-stone.

Painful indeed are the sorrows of separation.

Full of agitation, it was only natural that I wished to
cling to my dream.

Left entirely alone, I sadly sigh.

Oh, where now is my charming and precious beauty?'

The LUTE-BEARER *says:*

> The dawn has arrived. Let us at once proceed
> on another stage of our journey, and take some
> refreshment farther on.

MR. CHANG *sings:*

'The long branches of the weeping willow make sad
thoughts arise within me.

The gentle sound of the rippling water is like the
sobbing of my love.

The waning moon and the dying lamp are dim and
gradually fading.

My former sorrow and my new grief succeeding each
other, seem incurable.

My sadness at leaving and my regret at separation
    have so imbued my heart that they will ever be
    with me.
If I use not pen and paper instead of human voice,
To whom can I tell my innumerable thoughts of her
    whom I love?'   [*Exeunt.*

CONTINUATION

THE TITLES OF THE FOUR ACTS OF THE CONTINUATION OF 'THE WESTERN CHAMBER'

The LUTE-BEARER reports success at the examination.
TS'UI YING-YING sends a vest.
CHÊNG PAI-CH'AŇG vainly sacrifices his own life.
CHANG CHÜN-JUI's romance is happily ended.

ACT I

REPORT OF SUCCESS AT THE EXAMINATION

MR. CHANG *enters and says:*

> Half a year has passed since I parted last autumn from the Young Lady. Thanks to the protecting good fortune of my forebears, I have passed at the first attempt in the examination. I am now awaiting the final approval of the Imperial Pen. Being afraid that the Young Lady may be in a state of anxious expectation, I have written a special letter, which I will order my Lute-bearer to take to her, so that Madam and the Young Lady may know that I have passed and thus be relieved of their anxiety. The letter is ready, but where is the Lute-bearer?

The LUTE-BEARER *enters, and says:*

> What orders have you for me?

MR. CHANG *says:*

> Take this letter, travelling even by night, to the Prefecture of Ho-chung. When you see the Young Lady, tell her that your master, being afraid that she is anxious, has specially sent you in the first instance to take this letter to her.

He sings:

> 'When we last met the red petals of the flowers were falling like rain on the green moss.
> After we had separated, the faded leaves lay scattered in the evening mist.

To-day the plum-blossoms are seen,
And, to my surprise, a half-year has gone,
So especially a letter I send.'

He says:

My Lute-bearer, after you have conveyed to her
my news, you must ask for a reply and return as
quickly as possible.   [*Exit.*

The LUTE-BEARER *says:*

With this letter I am about to make a journey by
night and day to the Prefecture of Ho-chung.
                    [*Exit.*

YING-YING *enters with* HUNG NIANG *and says:*

It is already half a year since Mr. Chang went to
the Capital, and no news of any kind has up to the
present been received from him. For some time
I have been very uneasy in mind and have been
disinclined to use my mirror or attend to my toilet.
My figure is wasting, and my red skirt is too loose.
How sorrowful and sad I have become!

She sings:

'Although my sorrow is not revealed in my eyes,
Grief is still in my heart.
And even if it could leave my heart
It would always remain in my knitted eyebrows.
When I try to forget it,
It returns again as before.
My sad thoughts of him are never ceasing.
How can the small space of my eyebrows
Bear so many painful frowns?
New sorrows recently have followed old sorrows,
And they have become so confused that it is difficult
    to distinguish the new from the old.

The old sorrows are like the great mountain T'ai Hang,
dimly perceived,
While the new sorrows are like the great river Yangtze,
which flows on for ever.'

HUNG NIANG *says:*

My Young Mistress, when formerly you have been
out of sorts, a short rest has always done you good,
but I have never seen you so terribly wasted as
you are now.

YING-YING *sings:*

'When previously I have been wasting away,
I have always been able to find some relief.
But this time the affair is so very serious
That I can find no way of forgetting my sorrow.
Alone I enter my boudoir,
Roll up the curtains of beads and hang them on their
hooks of jade.
With listless gaze I see the clear hills and beautiful
water,
The trees enveloped in grey mist,
And decayed grass as far as the eye can reach,
While a boat lies alongside the ferry in the wilds.'

She says:

My clothes seem now as if they do not belong to me.

HUNG NIANG *says:*

My Young Mistress, your figure has become too
frail for your clothes.

YING-YING *sings:*

'My skirt, in colour like the pomegranate flower,
Has been creased in its red folds when I slept.
My buttons, in form like lilac,

221

'WITH LISTLESS GAZE I SEE THE CLEAR HILLS AND BEAUTIFUL WATER,
THE TREES ENVELOPED IN GREY MISTS,

'AND DECAYED GRASS AS FAR AS THE EYE CAN REACH,
WHILE A BOAT LIES ALONGSIDE THE FERRY IN THE WILDS'

More than meet the button-holes shaped like hibiscus
  flowers.
Resembling precious pearls that have become un-
  threaded,
My tears fall incessantly on my fragrant silk sleeves.
My eyebrows, shaped like the leaves of the willow, are
  knitted.
I am even thinner than the stem of a chrysanthemum.'

The LUTE-BEARER *enters and says:*
> I have received the orders of my master to bring
> a letter for the Young Lady. I have just seen her
> mother in the front hall, who was very delighted
> and told me to come in to see the Young Lady.
> I have now arrived at the back hall. (*He coughs.*)

HUNG NIANG *says:*
> Who is it?

She, seeing the LUTE-BEARER, *smiles and says:*
> When did you arrive? My Young Mistress is in
> great distress. Have you come by yourself, or
> have you come with your master?

The LUTE-BEARER *says:*
> My master has obtained an official post. He has
> ordered me to come first with this letter to tell
> you the good news.

HUNG NIANG *says:*
> You just wait here. After I have told my Young
> Mistress, you may come in.

She sees YING-YING, *and smilingly says:*
> Congratulations, my Young Mistress! Congratu-
> lations! Mr. Chang has obtained an official post.

YING-YING *says:*

> You little minx! Seeing me in distress, you only
> want to humbug me.

HUNG NIANG *says:*

> The Lute-bearer is at the door. He has seen your
> mother, who has told him to come in to see you.

YING-YING *says:*

> Though I should be ashamed to say it, the day
> for which I have longed on his behalf has at last
> arrived.

> (*The* LUTE-BEARER *meets* YING-YING.)

YING-YING *says:*

> Lute-bearer, when did you leave the Capital?

The LUTE-BEARER *says:*

> About a month ago. When I was leaving, my
> master was going about the streets having a merry
> time.

YING-YING *says:*

> You silly creature! You don't know that he who
> has gained the highest place at the examination
> has to go round the streets for three days, and this
> is called "To display the honour he has acquired'.

The LUTE-BEARER *says:*

> What you say is right, my Young Lady. Here is
> the letter.

YING-YING *sings:*

'Ever since his departure
My gay spirits have almost disappeared.
And even if you have sent a letter,
It can only increase my sorrow.
You have not proved true to the words you spoke.

I hang down my head in silence,
With the letter in my hand,
And my eyes full of tears.

Here I open the letter in tears,
There he wrote it also in tears.
It may be that tears flowed from his eyes before he had
    written it and made him put down his pen.
Now that he has sent it here, the stains of tears are still
    visible,
And the old stains of his tears are submerged in the
    new stains of mine.
This is indeed a sorrow's crown of sorrow.'

She reads the letter, which says:

Chang Kung makes his bows and presents this
letter to his fair and sweet lady. Since he, last
autumn, bade her farewell, half a year has suddenly
passed. By the blessed protection of his ancestors
and the virtues of his worthy spouse, he has been
fortunate enough to pass among the first three
on the examination list. Now he is temporarily
residing in the 'Hall of Worthies', awaiting promotion to office. Being afraid that Madam and
his worthy Spouse may be feeling anxious, he has
specially ordered his Lute-bearer to convey this
letter to report at once. Although he is absent in
body, his heart is always with her. He regrets that
he and she cannot be with each other like two
love-birds flying side by side, or two griffins gallop-
ing together. Please do not blame him too severely
for stressing too much the honour he has gained
and treating too lightly his love for her and he
will be profoundly grateful. If she will allow him
to speak of his feelings since their separation, they
will be entirely conveyed to her when they meet.

226

Attached is a short poem presented for her of such clear intelligence.

'The Third on the List at the Jewel Capital of Fairy-land,

Sends word to tell the very beautiful Lady of P'u Tung,

That he will soon obtain special leave from the Emperor and return at once in fine official array,

So that she may now cease to lean on the door, longing for his return.'

YING-YING *says:*

What a shame! They have only made him the Third on the list.

She sings:

'Formerly he concealed himself by moonlight in the Western Chamber;

To-day he is a guest of honour at the Imperial Banquet to celebrate his literary success.

He, who jumped over a wall, has now become one of the foremost scholars.

He, of the flower heart, who loved so dearly, has plucked the cassia branch from the moon.

He, who was so immersed in love of rouge and powder, has shown that in his heart is true refinement.

From now henceforward, my private boudoir will become the abode of a great official.'

She asks the LUTE-BEARER:

Have you had your meal yet?

The LUTE-BEARER *says:*

Not yet.

YING-YING *says:*

> Hung Niang, go at once to get something for him to eat.

The LUTE-BEARER *says:*

> While I am taking my meal, please, Young Lady, write a letter at once, because my master instructed me to get an answer and return as quickly as possible.

YING-YING *says:*

> Hung Niang, bring me pen and paper.
>
> (*She writes a letter.*)

YING-YING *says:*

> My letter is written. I have really nothing worthy to show my feelings, but I am sending him an inner garment, a belt, a pair of stockings, a lute, a jade hair-pin, and a pen of spotted bamboo. Lute-bearer, pack these things carefully. Hung Niang, give him ten taels of silver for his travelling expenses.

HUNG NIANG *says:*

> Now Mr. Chang has become an official, is he not sure to have those things, so why send them to him?

YING-YING *says:*

> How can you know what is at the bottom of my heart? Listen, and I will tell you.

She sings:

> 'As to the inner garment,
> If he uses it as a night-dress
> It will be as if he and I were together.
> And with it wrapped around his person
> He cannot but think of my tenderness.

As for the belt,
It will encircle him in front and behind,
And protect him, right and left,
And will be bound near his heart.
As to the stockings,
They will secure him from wandering astray.

As for the lute,
Formerly we sought each other with our poems;
Afterwards, with the aid of a seven-stringed lute, our
    union was effected.
How can he neglect the sentiments expressed in the
    poems?
All I fear is that the hand that played on the lute may
    become unpractised.
As to the jade hair-pin,
I have a special reason for sending it.
Now that he has attained his high honours
I fear that I may be put at the back of his mind (like a
    hair-pin that is placed at the back of the head).
As for the spotted bamboo pen,
In autumn, on either bank of the river Hsiang bamboos
    grew,
And as the Empress O Huang stained them with her
    tears of sorrow for the death of her husband the
    Emperor Shun,
So I, Ying-ying, to-day am filled with feelings of like
    devotion for my beloved Chün-jui.
Like those bamboos at the foot of the Chiu Ying
    Mountain,
The sleeves of my fragrant silk gown

Are wet with tears,
And stained as the bamboos of old.

The causes of grief are manifold, but the sorrow arising
    is ever the same.
Tears follow each other,
And regret and sorrow are never ending.
Tell him, the Scholar, the reasons of my gifts,
And that he must never forget his first love.'

The LUTE-BEARER *says:*

    I will carry out your instructions.

YING-YING *says:*

    Lute-bearer, have those things carefully packed.

She sings:

'As you proceed on your journey at night-time, rest in
    an inn,
But do not make the parcel with my gifts in it your
    pillow,
In case the grease from your hair should stain them
    beyond repair.
If soaked with water or wetted with rain, do not rinse it,
For fear that after they are dried the creases cannot be
    ironed out.
With each one of my gifts
Take a special care.

The letter to be sent is now finished,
But when will the love of my heart ever end?
The Capital where he is seems as far off as the heavens.
From every corner of the Western Tower I have looked
    for him,
But I only see the water flowing by while he comes not.'

The LUTE-BEARER *says:*

    Your servant bids you, my Young Lady, farewell
    and will now leave.

YING-YING *says:*

> Lute-bearer, when you see your master tell him . . .

LUTE-BEARER *says:*

> What shall I tell him?

YING-YING *sings:*

> 'He, on one side, is pining for me,
> While I, on my side, am wasting away on his account.
> When he was about to depart, his crafty tongue misled
> me
> By promising to return on the ninth of the Ninth Moon,
> But already the Tenth Moon has passed.
> Now I regret that I ever induced him to seek high
> rank.'

The LUTE-BEARER *says:*

> Having got the reply, I will now take it back,
> travelling night and day.

> > > > [*Exit.*

> > > [*Exeunt* YING-YING *and* HUNG NIANG.

ACT II

GUESSING THE MEANING OF HER GIFTS

Mr. Chang *enters, and says:*

I was full of hope that after my promotion to office I should be able at once to leave the Capital. But quite unexpectedly I have received an Imperial Decree appointing me to be a Compiler of National History in the Imperial College of Literature. Who can know the feelings of my heart? How can I accomplish any literary work? My Lute-bearer, who has gone with my message, has not yet returned. Not having been able to sleep comfortably or eat and drink with relish for several days, I have been given leave to rest in the official hostel. This morning a physician from the Imperial Medical Institution was sent to see me and give me medicine. But my sickness is one that not even the most famous of doctors could cure. Since I have been separated from my Young Lady, my heart has not had one day's ease!

He sings:

'Since my arrival at the Capital,
My loving thoughts of her have been the same morning
   and night,
And my heart has always been full of my Ying-ying.
The doctor was called in,
And after he had examined me
He told me exactly what my case is.
Although my wish was to treat the matter evasively,

232

He had already discovered the truth,
And no further examination on his part was necessary.

He said that other diseases had their remedies,
But that lovesickness no medicine could cure.
O my Young Lady!
If you but knew how my love for you makes me suffer.
I would willingly die for you—yes, die for you!
A wanderer at large without home,
A lonely stranger in a foreign land,
Have I been for almost half a year.'

The LUTE-BEARER *enters, and says:*

When I came back and made inquiries I was told
that my master was ill in the official hostel. I must
hand him the reply.

(*He sees* MR. CHANG.)

MR. CHANG *says:*

My Lute-bearer, so you have returned.

He sings:

'On the branch with blossoms sings the bird of happy
omen;
On the curtain is suspended the lucky spider;
Last night the lamp on the low stand burst into a
sparkling flame, betokening good fortune.
It must be, in one form or another, a poem showing
her heart-broken feelings.
When she wrote it, it is certain that her tears of love
fell like rain;
Otherwise how could the envelope be marked with the
stains of her tears?'

233

He reads the letter, which says:

Your ill-fated handmaid, Ts'ui, makes her bow in reply to the literary presence of the talented scholar Chün-jui. We have been separated for more than half a year, which really has seemed more than three years. My longing for you has suffered no abatement. As the old saying has it: 'The Sun seems near as compared with the distance of the Capital.' And now I realize the truth of that saying. The Lute-bearer has arrived, and I have received your letter. I learn from it that you have gained lofty promotion, and know that all is well with you. This being the case, what more need I say? As the Lute-bearer has to return at once, I have really nothing by which to express my feelings, so I can only send you a lute, a jade hair-pin, a spotted bamboo pen, a belt, an inner garment, and a pair of silk stockings. Although these articles are quite insignificant and unworthy, I hope you will be pleased to accept them all. The wind in spring is very keen, so take every care of your precious self. Further, I respectfully send you a poem in the same rhyme as that received from you:

'Leaning on the balustrade, I look longingly for the talented Scholar,
Who must not dwell on the attraction of any fair beauty at the Capital.
When sick I received your letter telling me that you had attained a high degree,
In front of the window I look into my glass to try my new toilet.'

Oh, how romantic my Young Lady is! For such

a maid as this I, Chang Kung, might well give up my life!

He sings:

'Such handwriting as hers is worthy of a calligraphist,
And of being inscribed on precious articles.
It has the power of the handwriting of Lui K'ung-ch'uan,
And the strength of that of Yen Chên-ch'ing.
Like Chang Hsü, Chang Tzu, Wang Hsi-chih, and
   Wang Hsien-chih,
The finest calligraphists of their time, she is the finest
   of to-day.
The literary talent of my Fair Lady,
My Ying-ying, is second to none in this world.

I will regard it as a sacred book,
And use it as a charm.
It is as precious and valuable as a gold ornament or
   gold tissue or gold itself.
If it were duly signed, and an official were made to
   dispatch a messenger with it,
It would be regarded, without an official seal,
As a summons to be obeyed at once.'

He looks at the inner garment and says:

To say nothing of her literary style, just look at this inner garment she has sent!

He sings:

'How could you fail to make me love you!
It is worthy to give her needlework special fame,
And to make her the model teacher of her sex.
Innumerable as are the thoughts which she has be-
   stowed on it, every one has proved to be excellent,
As I myself can easily perceive.

235

She had no model showing how long or how short it
    should be,
And she had to use her imagination as to the dimensions
    of my waist.
She had no one on whom to try it.
I feel that when she was making it she gave to it all
    her dear little heart.'

He says:

    All the articles that the Young Lady has sent have
    a meaning, which I have guessed in each case.

He sings:

    'The lute is to instruct me within closed door to
        practise the fingering,
    To pay attention to making the poem into a musical
        score,
    To nourish a mind like that of the holy worthies of old,
    And to keep my ears pure for musical sounds.

    The jade hair-pin is thin and long like a bamboo shoot,
    Delicate and white like an onion stalk,
    Beautifully soft and smooth,
    Lustrous and pure without a flaw.

    The spotted pen is like a frosted branch on which the
        male and female phoenix might perch,
    And is bedewed with tears mingled with rouge.
    Of old, the death of the Emperor Shun made his consort
        O Huang weep,
    And to-day my gentle maiden is thinking of her hero.

    The belt is made by holding in her hand a piece of
        cotton

236

And plying her needle to and fro, again and again,
    beneath the lamp,
Thus showing the sorrow of her mind,
And being in unison with the feelings of her heart.

The stockings have stitches as minute as small insects,
And silk lining as soft as goose-fat.
As I know what is propriety and will not act wrongly,
, She wishes that my feet will always follow that course.'

He says:

    My Lute-bearer, when you were about to depart,
    what did the Young Lady say to you?

The LUTE-BEARER *says:*

    She told me to tell you, my Master, that you must
    not on any account enter into another matrimonial
    engagement.

MR. CHANG *says:*

    Oh, my Young Lady! You still do not know my
    heart!

He sings:

'Very lonely am I in this inn.
The wind comes in gusts.
And the rain keeps falling.
The rain drips, the wind lightly blows, and I awake
    from my dreams.
How full of sorrow my heart is!

I seem to have lost control of my arms and legs.
My ability to reach the monastery of P'u Tung fills
    me with anxiety.
My Young Lady, when you see me

What will you have to tell me?
I am a young gallant and a romantic scholar.
How could I ever be willing to take a damaged flower
    or to pluck a stalk that is not fresh?
Ever since I have been here, never have I wandered
    about the streets!

Very seldom indeed is there the family of a Prime
    Minister
With a beautiful and charming daughter seeking for a
    son-in-law.
But even granted that there might be a charmer like you,
Where can one be found with such tenderness and such
    talents as yours?
How can the thought of Ying-ying
Fail to make one dwell upon her in dreams and in sleep?

Go to my library and empty a rattan box there,
And spread a few sheets of paper inside.
Be careful when you put in the things,
So that the pricks of the rattan may not puncture the
    cotton and silk.
If they are hung and spread on the clothes-rack,
I am afraid the wind will affect their colour;
And if they are carelessly kept in a bundle,
I am afraid their folds will be creased.
You must act as I tell you,
Take every care
And not be remiss!

Before we parted I was as happy as a newly married man;
But now I have arrived in search of literary honour
At the Capital, my thoughts are far away at the monas-
    tery of P'u Tung.

It seemed but last night that the peach and plum
　　flowers were blooming in the spring wind,
While to-day the leaves are falling from the *sterculia*
　　tree in the autumn rain.
Amidst such sad surroundings,
Though I am absent in the flesh, my heart is with
　　her,
And whether I rest or move my thoughts are ever
　　of her.

Our love, lofty as Heaven and stable as Earth,
Will last till the sea runs dry and the rocks are melted
　　away.
When will my thoughts of her cease?
They are like the candle, the tears of which will only
　　cease to flow after it has been reduced to ashes;
And like the silkworm, which will only cease to spin
　　when its life ends.
I am not to be compared with the fickle gallant
Who, regardless of the harmony between husband and
　　wife,
Separates the male and female phoenix.

No word of news was brought to me by "The Yellow
　　Dog",
And it was impossible for her to send to me a love
　　poem on a "Red Leaf".
The road was long, and no messenger with the Plum
　　Blossom was to be found.
I was a lonely wanderer in a strange land, three thousand
　　miles from home.
For twenty-four hours a day I kept thinking of my
　　return.
Leaning on the balustrade I watched,

And all I heard was the loud rushing sound of the river,
And all I saw was the different hues of the mountains.

Sad though I be in my sickness,
Happy indeed am I since your letter has come.
It has taken possession of my soul, and is like that of
     Cho-Wên-chün,
Which had nearly killed her lover, Ssŭ-ma Hsiang-ju,
     with longing for its arrival.'   [*Exeunt.*

ACT III

THE CONTEST FOR THE BEAUTY

CHÊNG HÊNG *enters, and says:*

My surname is Chêng, my name is Hêng, and my style is Pai-ch'ang. My late father was appointed the President of the Board of Rites. When he was alive he betrotheu me to Ying-ying, the daughter of my paternal aunt. Unexpectedly my aunt's husband died and Ying-ying had to go into mourning for her father. As the period of mourning has not yet ended, our marriage has not been carried out. My aunt, along with Ying-ying, is conveying my uncle's coffin back to Po-ling to be buried there. Having been stopped on her journey, she is staying temporarily in the Prefecture of Ho-chung. Several months ago she sent a letter to tell me to go to her. But as there was no one to look after my family I have delayed my coming. To my surprise, when I arrived here, I heard that Sun, the Flying Tiger, wanted to carry off Ying-ying, but that a scholar, Chang Chün-jui by name, succeeded in making the bandit-soldiers retire. My aunt then betrothed Ying-ying to him. If I were now to intrude I am afraid it would not look well. This affair now depends entirely upon the maid Hung Niang, so I sent some one to call upon her and simply to say that I have just come from the Capital and dare not too suddenly visit my aunt. I also told her to come up to my place as I have something which I want her to tell my aunt.

My messenger has been away for some time. Why has not Hung Niang come yet?

HUNG NIANG *enters and says:*

Mr. Chêng Hêng is staying at a lodging, but has not come to see my Mistress. He summoned me to have a talk with him, and my Mistress told me to come to hear what he has to say.

(HUNG NIANG *sees* CHÊNG.)

HUNG NIANG *says:*

Ten thousand blessings on you, sir. My Mistress says, since you have arrived, why don't you go to her house?

CHÊNG *says:*

How can I possibly go to see my aunt? I have sent for you in order to tell you about my uncle having betrothed me when he was alive. Now I have arrived here, and, the period of mourning for my uncle having expired, I specially request you to go to inform my aunt, so that she may select a lucky day for accomplishing our happy union, and then afterwards we may all go together to have the coffin buried. The postponement of our union would not matter very much, but great inconvenience might otherwise arise on the journey. If you are able to persuade her to consent I will reward you very handsomely.

HUNG NIANG *says:*

You must not again refer to the matter of the union, because Ying-ying is already betrothed to Mr. Chang.

CHÊNG *says:*

Don't you know that one horse cannot have two saddles? Her father when alive betrothed her to me. Now that he is dead how can his widow go back on her husband's promise? Who ever heard of such a principle?

HUNG NIANG *says:*

The case is not as you put it. When Sun, the Flying Tiger, came with five thousand bandit-soldiers where were you then, sir? If it had not been for Mr. Chang, how could the whole family have escaped with their lives? To-day, when complete peace reigns, you come to contend for the Young Lady. Supposing the bandits had carried her off, with whom would you have pleaded your suit, sir?

CHÊNG *says:*

If she were given to some rich family that would not be such an outrageous *mésalliance*. But to give her to such a poor starved wretch, as if I were not as good as he! How can he for a moment be compared with me, a man of the highest virtue and sprung from well-known stock?

HUNG NIANG *says:*

Not as good as you! You hold your tongue!

She sings:

'You boast of your high virtues
And rely on your well-known stock;
But even if you go on receiving promotion after promotion
Who would promise to let you become one of the family?
Besides, no go-between has been engaged, no betrothal presents in the form of kids and geese have passed,
Nor have silks been sent to ask the consent of the bridal family.

Now that you have only just removed the dust of your
  journey
You want the maiden to marry you at once.
You will thus profane her Golden Boudoir and Silver
  Screen;
You will begrime her silken coverlet and embroidered
  bedding.

You will be unworthy of her locks, like clouds, and of
  her chignon, made up in the shape of the moon;
You will be a disgrace to one so tender and beautiful;
You will pollute her romance.
When the three Primordial Forces (Heaven, Earth, and
  Man) were first divided,
When the Male and Female Principles were first
  separated
Into Heaven and Earth,
The pure part became Heaven,
The dense part became Earth,
And Man was between the two.
Chün-jui is a pure worthy,
While Chêng Hêng is a dense creature.'

CHÊNG *says:*
  When the bandits came, how could he make them
  retreat? The whole thing is nonsense.

HUNG NIANG *says:*
  Listen, and I will tell you.

She sings:
  'Guarding Ho Chiao, the Flying Tiger General
  Revolted at P'u Tung, and plundered the people.
  With five thousand bandit soldiers he besieged the
  monastery.

With a glittering sword in his hand
He shouted aloud, saying:
"I must have Ying-ying as the mistress of the camp."'

CHÊNG *says:*

> What could he do single-handed against five
> thousand bandit soldiers?

HUNG NIANG *says:*

> The siege of the monastery by the bandits having
> become very critical, my Mistress was full of fear
> and consulted with the Superior, who was told to
> call aloud: 'He who, whether priest or layman,
> can make the bandits retire, will be given Ying-
> ying as wife.' Then Mr. Chang responded, say-
> ing: 'I have a plan for making the bandits to retire.
> Why not consult me about it?' My Mistress,
> highly delighted, inquired what the plan might be.
> Mr. Chang said: 'I have an old friend, the General
> of the White Horse, who is now in command of a
> hundred thousand fine troops, guarding the P'u
> Pass. I will write a letter and send a messenger
> with it. He is sure to come to my rescue.' Who
> would have thought that immediately on the
> arrival of the letter the troops were dispatched and
> the critical situation was at once relieved?

She sings:

'The brilliant Scholar of Lo-yang, so skilled in literature,
Wrote a letter at lightning speed.
The moment the General of the White Horse arrived
The cloud and smoke of the siege were extinguished,
The minds of my Mistress and her daughter were set
    at ease.
Because he was powerful but not ruthless,

245

And was true to his word,
We could not presume to treat him disrespectfully.'

CHÊNG *says:*

> I have never even heard of his name before; how could I know anything about his prowess? You little minx, why are you trying to bluff me by making so much of him?

HUNG NIANG *sings:*

> 'As he is a philosopher of the Confucian school,
> A poet and a prose-writer in the style of Han Yü and Liu Tsung-yüan,
> And a moralist who knows the principles of human conduct,
> We must act with sincerity
> And return good for good.'

CHÊNG *says:*

> In what way am I not his equal?

HUNG NIANG *sings:*

> 'Supposing you are one per cent,
> He is a hundred per cent.
> How can a mere fire-fly be compared with the full moon?
> Putting aside all questions of superiority and inferiority,
> I will give you the letters which will show the difference between the excellence of him and the worthlessness of you:
> Chün-jui is c-h-a-r-m-i-n-g,
> Whilst you are a s-i-l-l-y a-s-s!'

CHÊNG *says:*

> S-i-l-l-y a-s-s? Do you mean that I am really a silly ass? Am I, whose family, for generations,

have been officials, not worthy of comparison with
a mere nobody, a wretched student?

HUNG NIANG *sings:*

'He, following the teachings of his master and friends,
Is a gentleman who is devoted to the foundations of life,
You, depending on your forebears and elders,
Use your influence to oppress people
He lived on the humblest fare for days and months
  without grumbling at his poverty,
And gained new fame and renown by his own efforts.

You wretch, your views are entirely false.
And you know not the difference between right and
  wrong.
You say that only official families are worthy of being
  official,
And you readily utter such nonsense
Which is opposed to the true facts.
You say the poor always remain poor,
Instead of that Prime Ministers and Generals are
  produced from the homes of the poor.'

CHÊNG *says:*

This whole affair is the work of Fa Pên, that bald
ass of a Buddhist novitiate! I will thrash out the
matter with him to-morrow.

HUNG NIANG *sings:*

'He, who has left his family to become a priest, has
  charity and pity as his guiding principles,
And good works for others as his doctrine.
Your eyes, which show that you will have an unhappy
  ending, do not know a good man when they see
  him;

247

And your mouth, which will bring you disaster, does not know when to restrain itself.'

CHÊNG *says:*

My betrothal was the dying command of my uncle, so I will choose a day, bring the sheep, and carry the wine to her door, and see how my aunt deals with me.

HUNG NIANG *sings:*

'You abusive, foul-mouthed bully!
What do you know about gentility or politeness?
You want to obtain your matrimonial object by might,
And, regardless of all consequences, to effect a forced union.'

CHÊNG *says:*

If my aunt rejects me, I will get twenty or thirty of my associates to carry the Young Lady into the chair, take her to my place, there disrobe her, and soon return her to you as a married lady.

HUNG NIANG *sings:*

'You, who are the direct descendant of the Minister Chêng,
Are behaving as if you were a rough soldier, bred in the camp of Sun, the Flying Tiger.
You ugly, dirty, corpse-like creature,
Nothing can save you from being a homeless vagabond.'

CHÊNG *says:*

Oh, you little minx! It is quite obvious that you have surrendered to the other party. I will not talk to you any more. To-morrow I will marry her—will marry her!

248

HUNG NIANG *says:*

> She will not marry you—will not marry you!

She sings:

'The fair lady is in love with one who is charming and
    attractive.
Even if I were told not to sing his praises
How could I possibly refrain?
You are only worthy to play second fiddle to Han Shou
    by trying to follow his lead;
And no powder could make your face beautiful like that
    of Mr. Ho.'   [*Exit.*

CHÊNG *says:*

> That little minx has most certainly been carrying
> on with that wretched creature! When I go to-
> morrow to the house to see my aunt I will pretend
> to be entirely ignorant. I will only say that Mr.
> Chang has become the son-in-law of the family of
> President Wei. My aunt, who loves gossip, is sure
> to have something to say. To mention nothing
> else, this suit of mine will be sufficient to attract
> her in my favour.

He sings:

'When I was young, we lived together in the Capital,
And I was well versed in composing essays and poems.
My uncle has already betrothed me,
So who dares to find excuses to put off my suit?
If I put on a bold face,
I should like to see to whom else Ying-ying can go!
My cunning, which I always use to oppress the good
    and bully the worthy,
Will now be employed for the time being to effect our
    happy union.'   [*Exit.*

MADAM *enters, and says:*

> Last night Chêng Hêng arrived, but instead of coming to see me he sent for Hung Niang to inquire about the marriage. According to my view, the right thing to do is to give my daughter to my nephew. Besides, when my husband was alive, she was already betrothed to him. If I act contrary to my late husband's instructions I will be proceeding improperly as the head of the family. Prepare the feast, as he will probably come to see me to-day.

CHÊNG HÊNG *enters, and says:*

> I have arrived and I will walk in unannounced.
>
> (*He weeps, and bows to* MADAM.)

MADAM *says:*

> My child, having arrived here, why did you not come at once to see me?

CHÊNG *says:*

> How could I have the face to come to see you, my aunt?

MADAM *says:*

> Ying-ying, on account of the Flying Tiger affair, had no means of getting out of the danger, so was betrothed to Mr. Chang.

CHÊNG *says:*

> What Mr. Chang? Is it he who has just passed third on the list at the recent examination? When I was in the Capital I saw the list. He is about twenty-three or twenty-four years of age. He comes from Lo-yang, and his name is Chang Kung. He paraded the streets for three days to show the honours he had acquired. On the second day he came straight to the entrance of the residence of

the President, Wei. The President's daughter, in an ornamental pavilion, erected on the Imperial Road, hit him with an embroidered ball. I was also riding a horse and looking on, and the ball almost hit me. About ten maids, used for rough work by the family, seized Mr. Chang, and pulled him off his horse and dragged him in, heels first. He cried out loudly: 'I have already a wife of my own. I am the son-in-law of the Prime Minister Ts'ui.' But how could the President agree to listen to him? So the President said: 'My daughter, by Imperial Decree, had this ornamental pavilion erected to invite you to become the son-in-law of the family. As for your Ying-ying, she first surrendered herself before her marriage, and is therefore only fit to be a secondary wife. On this account the Capital was thrown into an uproar, and it was in this way that I got to know about him.

MADAM, *in fury, says:*

I always said that this student was not worthy of being exalted to our family, and to-day he has indeed proved false to our family. How could the daughter of a Prime Minister ever possibly become a secondary wife! Since Mr. Chang has made another marriage we will have nothing more to do with him. You, my child, may select a lucky day and a fortunate hour, and, as originally arranged, become my son-in-law. [*Exit.*

CHÊNG, *full of joy, says:*

She has fallen into my trap! I will at once get ready presents and rewards for my marriage.
[*Exit.*

ACT IV

THE GLORIOUS HOME-COMING

Fa Pên, *the Superior, enters, and says:*

Yesterday I bought a register of the successful candidates at the Examination, and found that Mr. Chang has passed, and has been appointed the Prefect of Ho-chung. Who would have thought that Madam, who is so uncertain in her views, would have promised her daughter to Chêng Hêng and is unwilling to receive Mr. Chang? I have prepared a feast, which I am taking to the Farewell Pavilion to welcome the returning official.

[*Exit.*

General Tu *enters, and says:*

By Imperial Decree, I have been ordered to take command of soldiers at the P'u Pass, and to be in charge of military affairs in Ho-chung Prefecture. To my surprise, my sworn brother, Chün-jui, has succeeded in his first attempt in the highest examination and has been appointed the Prefect of Ho-chung. He is sure to avail himself of this opportunity to complete his marriage. I am going with presents of sheep and wine to the residence of Madam Ts'ui, on the one hand to offer her my congratulations, and on the other to act as master of the marriage ceremonies. Attendants, bring my horse here. I am going to pay a visit to the Ho-chung Prefecture. [*Exit.*

Madam *enters, and says:*

Who would have thought it? Mr. Chang has

252

played our family false and has become the son-in-law of the President, Wei. So I will not disregard the dying instructions of my late husband and will make Chêng Hêng my son-in-law. To-day, being a lucky one for the marriage, I will get ready the feast. Chêng Hêng may be here any moment.

MR. CHANG *enters, and says:*

Having received, by Imperial Decree, the appointment of Prefect of Ho-chung, I have returned to-day in glory. My Young Lady will now have to wear her phoenix head-dress and red veil, which, when I see her, I will present with both hands. Who would have thought that to-day would at last arrive?

'My literary ability has for long been unequalled in the world,

But now my name has become universally known.'

He sings:

'Whip in hand, on a spirited steed, I leave the Royal Capital,

Being as full of romance as I am of learning.

To-day I am the possessor of the Third Rank,

Yesterday I was but a poor student!

The Imperial Pen has just promoted me,

By marking my name as a member of the Imperial Academy.

Chang Kung, as Yen Hui, may look like a fool,

But he has fulfilled his ambition by revealing his flashing brilliance, resembling that of the long-hidden sword Lung Ch'üan, and his knowledge of innumerable books.

253

Fortune has smiled upon Ying-ying,
Who is bound to receive the Five Flowered Patent of
　　Rank and the beautiful and honourable "Chariot
　　of the Seven Fragrances".
Now, in my glory, I cannot forget my having been
　　allowed to dwell in the monastery,
Nor will I cease to remember where in sorrow I wrote
　　my poem.
Ever since I went to attend the examinations
The memory of the road to P'u Tung has never been
　　absent even in my dreams.'

He arrives at the monastery, and says:
　　Take my horse.

He sees MADAM, *bows, and says:*
　　Chang Kung, who has just passed Third on the
　　List of the highest examination, Prefect of Ho-
　　chung, makes his bow to Madam.

MADAM *says:*
　　Don't bow! Don't bow! You are the son-in-law
　　of another family who has received an Imperial
　　Decree. How can I be worthy of receiving a bow
　　from you?

MR .CHANG *sings:*
　　'I have come personally to inquire after you health.
　　Who has caused your kindly face to look so angry?
　　I perceive that even the maids and attendants are
　　　exchanging strange glances with each other.
　　Can it be that there is something wrong about me?'

He says:
　　When I was leaving, you, Madam, personally gave
　　me a farewell feast and were overwhelmed with

254

delight. But now, on my return, after I have been selected for and obtained office, you, contrary to what one might expect, show displeasure. What is the reason?

MADAM *says:*

What do you care now about our family? I would like to remind you of the saying: "The beginning may always be good, but seldom is there a good ending!' My only daughter, though she may be untidy in dress and ugly in appearance, had as father a Prime Minister. If it had not been for the coming of the bandits, how could you ever have had influence enough to gain an entry into our family? Now, suddenly, you have shown your utter disregard for her by actually having become the son-in-law of the family of President Wei. How can such a proceeding be justified?

MR. CHANG *says:*

Madam, from whom did you hear this? If such be really the case, may I no longer live under Heaven or on Earth and be the victim of the direst disease!

He sings:

'If it is said that there are maidens as beautiful as pictures,
It is true that the streets of the Capital are full of them.
But my mind always dwelt upon those who had been kind to me here.
So how could I be willing to seek an alliance elsewhere?
Have you not heard that "A gentleman is always true from first to last"?
So how could I be willing to forget those who had befriended me?

255

What rascally beast, out of wild jealousy,
Has come here to stir up trouble and to separate us?
Not being able to secure the Fair Lady,
He has never ceased to use his craftiness.
The man who came to say this is a rogue of the deepest
dye.
And sooner or later will suffer death by torture.'

MADAM *says:*

It was Chêng Hêng who told me. The embroidered ball hit your horse and you thus became
the son-in-law. If you don't believe me, call Hung
Niang and ask her.

HUNG NIANG *enters, and says:*

I am more than anxious to see him. So he has come
back after having obtained office. What a shame!
The truth will now be known!

MR. CHANG, *questioning her, says:*

Hung Niang, how is your Young Mistress?

HUNG NIANG *says:*

As you have become the son-in-law of President
Wei, my Young Mistress will, as originally
arranged, marry Chêng Hêng.

MR. CHANG *says:*

How could there be anything so extraordinary as
this?

He sings:

'How could the true lovers' tree spring from a dung-
heap
And how could the two fish with two eyes between
them swim in dirty mud?

I cannot understand how the "Records of True Love"
can be thus sullied!

Oh, Ying-ying, you are going to marry a dirty, greasy
monkey as a husband!

Oh, Hung Niang, you will have to serve a soot-
begrimed cat as master!

Oh, Mr. Chang, you will have a half-drowned rat as
brother-in-law!

This will be an outrage on our customs

And a serious injury to human relations.'

HUNG NIANG *sings:*

'I have come to pay my respects in answer to your call.

I am trying to keep down the anger of my heart.

Have you been happy since we parted?

Where does the new bride dwell?

And how does she really compare with my Young
Mistress?'

MR. CHANG *says:*

Are you also talking nonsense? The sufferings I
endured on account of your Young Mistress out-
siders may not know, but you know them only too
well. And now that I have been able to reach
what I hoped would be the happy day, how could
such unreasonable conduct as that of which I am
accused have taken place?

He sings:

'If I have a bride elsewhere

May I die on the spot!

How can I forget waiting for the moonlight in the
corridor?

How could I abandon my beloved lute-player and
companion?

After I had endured hell on earth,
And exerted myself almost to death,
We were just about able to become man and wife.
Now, armed with an imperially conferred patent of
   "Dame"
And the title of "The Official Lady",
With overwhelming joy and delight
I was about to hand them with both hands to her,
But she is opening a grave in which to bury me, unjustly
   accused.'

HUNG NIANG, *addressing her Mistress, says:*
   I said that Mr. Chang was not a man of that kind.
   Let us call my Young Mistress to come and question him herself. (*She calls.*) My Young Mistress, Mr. Chang has arrived. Come out; it will
   be best for you to question him.

YING-YING *enters, and says:*
   Here I am.
        (*She meets* MR. CHANG.)

MR. CHANG *says:*
   Have you been quite well since we parted, my
   Young Lady?

YING-YING *says:*
   A thousand blessings on you, sir!

HUNG NIANG *says:*
   Haven't you something to say to him, my Young
   Mistress?

YING-YING *sighs, and says:*
   What is there to be said?

She sings:

'When I did not see him
I had already prepared no end of things to say to him;
But now we have met
All is changed to nothing but long and deep sighs.
He has come post-haste,
While I am too shy to glance at him.
I long to unfold to him the sorrows of my heart,
But, on meeting him, I cannot find a word to say
Beyond wishing him every blessing.'

She says:

Mr. Chang, what wrong has our family done you?
You have abandoned me and become the son-in-
law of the family of President Wei. How can such
an action be justified?

MR. CHANG *says:*

Who told you this?

YING-YING *says:*

Chêng Hêng said this in the presence of my
mother.

MR. CHANG *says:*

My Young Lady, how can you listen to such a
beast as he is? Only Heaven can know what is in
my heart!

He sings:

'Ever since I left the east of P'u Prefecture
And arrived at the Capital
I have never even ventured to glance at any fair maiden
     I may have met.
Without rhyme or reason I have been accused of having
     married the daughter of President Wei.

If I have ever seen even her shadow
May my family perish and my house cease to exist!'

He says:

> This whole matter rests entirely on Hung Niang's
> shoulders. I will speak to her so as to provoke her
> and see what she has to say. (*To* HUNG NIANG:)
> I have been making inquiries and was told that
> you and your Young Mistress have written to
> Chêng Hêng, telling him to come here.

HUNG NIANG *says:*

> You fool! I ought never to have helped you to
> fulfil your wishes! You are treating me badly.

She sings:

> 'Mr. Chün-jui, you need not be anxious,
> And there is no reason why you should worry.
> That creature is an absolute fool!
> Our family for generations has been upright and pure,
> Its forebears have always been worthy and good,
> And it has enjoyed the high reputation of having had
> a Prime Minister.
> How could any member of it condescend to write a
> letter to him?
>
> That creature, who deserves to be beaten,
> Is a dirty-mouthed rascal.
> He does not know black from white,
> And disfigures beauty with ugliness!
> Even allowing that my Young Mistress is weak and
> wavering,
> How could she marry such an utterly worthless shrimp
> and jade?
> She loves you as if you were the God of Spring,

And the Lord and Master of her who represents birds and flowers.

How could she be willing to allow her gentle stalk to be hacked by the axe of a common wood-cutter?

That creature's sole idea is to try to damage you by his craftiness.

I cannot say all I want to say

For my breast is bursting with fury!'

She says:

> Mr. Chang, if you have not really become the son-in-law of another family I will get my Mistress to do all in her power on your behalf. When that creature comes you and he can have it out with each other.

She reports to MADAM, *and says:*

> Mr. Chang has not become the son-in-law of another family. Chêng Hêng has told a pack of lies. Let them confront each other.

MADAM *says:*

> Since he *has* not, let Chêng Hêng come to confront him, and then we will see what is to be said.

FA PÊN *enters, and says:*

> To my surprise, Mr. Chang, having succeeded at the examination at his first attempt, has received the appointment of Prefect of Ho-chung. I have already welcomed him, and now I go to Madam to offer my congratulations. As to his marriage, I was, from the very beginning, concerned with it. Why has Madam proved so vacillating that she is actually preparing to give her daughter to Chêng Hêng? If she does give her to him, what is to happen when the Prefect comes to-day?

He meets all present, and says to MADAM:

> Now you know, Madam, that what I said was correct. Mr. Chang is definitely not a student of no character. How could he possibly forget you, Madam? General Tu was an eye-witness to this marriage arrangement, so how can you go back on it?

He sings:

> 'General Tu, who disdains Sun and P'ang as mere fools,
> And considers Chia and Ma as no heroes,
> Has just been appointed to be *Generalissimo* of the Western Punitive Expedition,
> And also to be in control of the Ho-chung Division in Shen-si.
>
> He, who formerly proved your protector,
> To-day, armed with authority and power,
> Is sure to help you when he arrives,
> And will be certain to punish the villain,
> Who, regardless of his relationship,
> Wants to cheat an honest man out of his wife.
> If you cannot distinguish a good man from a bad man
> You are not a hero; as the saying goes, "No man can be a hero unless he has some of the devil in him"!'

MADAM *says:*

> Take your Young Mistress to her bed-chamber.

> [*Exeunt* YING-YING *and* HUNG NIANG.

GENERAL TU *enters, and says:*

> I have left the P'u Pass and have just arrived at the P'u Chiu Monastery.

MR. CHANG, *having paid his respects to* GENERAL TU, *says:*

> By the powerful influence of you, my elder

brother, I have succeeded at the examinations. I have just returned, hoping to be married. But a nephew of Madam, named Chêng Hêng, came and told her that I had become the son-in-law of the family of President Wei. Madam was furious, wanted to go back on my marriage arrangements, and to give the Young Lady to Chêng Hêng as originally arranged. But, as is well known, 'A chaste girl never marries twice.'

GENERAL TU *says:*

Madam, you are wrong! My dear Chün-jui is not only the son of a President of the Board of Rites but has also succeeded in the examination. You, Madam, vowed that you would not have a son-in-law who has not passed such examinations, but now you want to cancel the marriage arrangement with him. Would not this be a most unjust proceeding?

MADAM *says:*

Originally, when my husband was alive, my daughter was betrothed to that fellow. But unexpectedly having fallen into a dangerous situation we were much indebted to Mr. Chang, who requested you to come to drive off the bandits. So I, according to my promise at that time, made him my son-in-law. But that fellow said that he had become the son-in-law of the family of President Wei. On account of this I was angry with him, and so wanted to give my daughter to Chêng Hêng as originally arranged.

GENERAL TU *says:*

He has the heart of a villain and is evidently falsely maligning Mr. Chang. How could you so easily believe him, Madam?

CHÊNG HÊNG *enters, and says:*

Here I am, arrayed to perfection, ready to become the son-in-law! To-day is a lucky day. Leading sheep and carrying wine, I am going to the house of the bride.

(*He meets all present.*)

MR. CHANG *says:*

Chêng Hêng, what has brought you here?

CHÊNG *says:*

Woe is me! Having heard that the First on the List of the examinations had returned, I have especially come to offer my congratulations.

GENERAL TU *says:*

You creature, how dare you try to swindle an honest man out of his wife, thus committing a most inhuman act? I will memorialize the throne to have this villain punished.

He sings:

'You want to force your way into Fairyland
Regardless of whom the master there may be!
But the God of Spring prevents the bee from approaching the flower.
Go to where the green willow casts its shade and listen to the nightjar
Which keeps on crying "You had better go home."'

He says:

If that creature does not clear out he will be arrested.

CHÊNG *says:*

It will not be necessary to arrest me, for I will give up my marriage in favour of Mr. Chang.

264

MADAM *says:*

> Calm your wrath, General. It will be sufficient to turn him out.

CHÊNG *says:*

> To-day Ying-ying and Chün-jui will become husband and wife. With what face can I return to see my own people? What use is life now to me? I had better kill myself by dashing out my brains against a tree.
>
> 'My vain struggle to obtain a wife has ended in failure.
> From of old a romantic hero cannot fail to be romantic.
> Of what use have been my various painful efforts and numerous schemes?
> All things come to an end at last, and now I perish for ever!'
>
> > (*He falls down dead.*)

MADAM *says:*

> Although he has not been forced by me to take his own life, out of pity for his being an orphan I will take charge of his burial.

GENERAL TU *says:*

> Ask the Young Lady to come out. To-day we will hold a congratulatory feast and see that the young couple are united.
>
> > (MR. CHANG *and* YING-YING *bow to* MADAM, *to each other, to* GENERAL TU; *and the maid*, HUNG NIANG, *bows to* MR. CHANG *and* YING-YING.)

OMNES:

> 'Four-horsed chariots crowd the gate,
> And eight young dragons adorn the door,

'THEY WILL LIVE UNDIVIDED FOR EVER UNTIL

OLD AGE, AND WILL BE TOGETHER FOR ETERNITY'

While you marry the Prime Minister's daughter, who
    has all the womanly virtues,
And thus fulfil the desire of your life,
Through the aid of your relations and friends.

Had it not been that your great benefactor had helped
    you by drawing his sword,
How could you have become husband and wife as happy
    as fish in water?
Fortunate indeed was the cause that first brought them
    together,
And it has now resulted in their being man and wife.
From of old a worthy maid is sure to mate a worthy
    husband,
The Third on the List, who has plucked the flower of
    success, is now about to tread the flowery path of
    love.'

        (*An* IMPERIAL MESSENGER *enters; all bow*.)

'Peace reigns throughout the world,
All the inhabitants of which proclaim themselves as
    loyal subjects.
All the various States come to pay their respects at the
    Court,
And the mountains re-echo as they exclaim "Long live
    the Emperor!"
His Majesty's deeds excel those of Fu Hsi and Huang Ti,
Like those of a sage are his plans and like that of a
    god is his penetration.
He is benevolent in his civil affairs and righteous in his
    military conquest.
The Prime Minister at the Court is worthy and good,
And the people under Heaven are prosperous.
The ten-thousand-mile River is untroubled,

And all the crops yield good harvests,
All households live in peace,
And everywhere is a happy land.
There are the happy auguries of the arrival of the
    phoenix,
And of the several appearances of the unicorn.

By the grace of the present sacred and wise Emperor
    of the T'ang Dynasty
A Decree has been issued sanctioning the marriage.
They will live undivided for ever until old age,
And will be together for eternity.
And we hope that all lovers throughout the whole world
    will be happily married.

Through having exchanged poems written under the
    moonlight,
They have ceased to be spinster and bachelor;
Which shows the high literary man of determination
    was bound to succeed,
As the ill-fated Chêng Hêng was doomed to failure.'

[*Exeunt.*

THE STORY OF TS'UI YING-YING

By YÜAN CHÊN (779–831 A.D.)

IN the Chen-yüan Period (A.D. 785–805) of the T'ang Dynasty, there was a Mr. Chang who was of a gentle and cultivated nature, of a very fine appearance, and of a firm and independent disposition. He was a stranger to anything in the nature of impropriety. When he joined with his friends in social amusements, and the fun became boisterous, whilst others revelled in it with enthusiasm as if they might miss their opportunity, Mr. Chang only made a show of joining in, but no one was able to make him lose his self-control. So when he reached the age of twenty-two he had never had anything to do with the fair sex. Those who knew of this fact asked him the reason. He excused himself by saying: "T'eng Tu was not a real admirer of beauty but merely a man of licentious behaviour. I am a real admirer of beauty but, as it happens, I have not yet met with a real beauty. May I further explain? Whenever I have met rare beauty of any kind it has never failed to remain imprinted on my heart. From which it can be known that I am not destitute of love of beauty." His interrogators noted his reply.

Soon after this Mr. Chang went to the district of P'u. To the east of which at a distance of more than ten li (li = one-third of a mile) there was a Buddhist temple called the P'u Chiu Monastery where Mr. Chang resided. It happened that the widow of the Ts'ui family, who was on her way back to Ch'ang-an (the Capital) passed through P'u on her journey and also had halted at that monastery. The widow Ts'ui was a daughter of the Cheng family, of which Mr. Chang was also a descendant. By tracing their relationship, he found her to be his aunt of a different branch (of the Cheng Clan). This year (General) Yun Hsien had died at P'u. His

271

immediate subordinate, Ting Wen-ya, had been unkind to the soldiers, so they availed themselves of the General's death to riot and plunder the people of P'u. The family of the widow Ts'ui had money and property of great value, and many servants. Being mere travellers in temporary residence, they were filled with alarm and did not know upon whom they could rely. Before this Mr. Chang had been on good terms with the friends of the Military Commandant of P'u. So he asked for official protection, and thus the trouble did not affect them. A little more than ten days afterwards the upright Commissioner, T'u Ch'ueh, came with an Imperial Edict authorizing him to be in complete control of military affairs. He issued orders to the soldiers, and so discipline was restored.

The widow Ts'ui was deeply grateful to Mr. Chang for his kindness, so she prepared a feast for him and entertained him in the middle hall, addressing him as follows: 'Your lonely widowed aunt, who has unjustly survived her husband, whilst taking her young children with her, has unfortunately met with a serious outbreak on the part of the soldiery, and would certainly never have been able to save herself. So that the lives of myself, my small son and young daughter, are due to you. How can this be compared with an ordinary favour! I will now make them pay their respects to you as their benefactor and elder brother in the hope that they may show some return for your benefaction.'

She first gave orders to her son, named Huan-lang, who was just over ten years old and very gentle and handsome in appearance. She then commanded her daughter, saying: 'Come forth and pay your respects to your elder brother. It is to him you owe your life.' After the lapse of a considerable time she asked to be excused on the plea of sickness. Her mother was angry and said: 'Your elder brother Chang has saved your life. Had it not been for this you would now be a captive. Can you still refuse to see him in order to avoid suspicions?' After a further lapse of time, she came, arrayed in ordinary attire and depressed in appearance, without having made herself up. Her locks hung loose, her black eyebrows were knitted, and the rouge on her cheeks had almost gone. Her appearance was extraordinarily beautiful and of a brilliance that would move any mortal. Mr. Chang, surprised, made his bow to her. She sat by the side of her mother and, on account of having been forced by her mother to come to the interview, with fixed gaze, she looked thoroughly distressed and as if she was about to collapse. When her age was asked her mother replied: 'She was born in the Seventh Moon of the Chia-tzu Year (A.D. 784) of the present Emperor, and is seventeen in this Keng ch'en Year (A.D. 800) of the Chengyüan Period.'

Mr. Chang tried to lead her into conversation, but she made no response, and so the feast came to an end. Mr. Chang was henceforward infatuated by her. He tried to let her know his sentiments, but found no means of being able to do so. The maidservant of the Ts'ui family was named Hung Niang, to whom Mr. Chang secretly made several polite salutations, and, having found an opportunity, he told her of his affection for her young mistress. Being greatly surprised and taken aback, she ran away hurriedly. Mr. Chang regretted what he had done. The following day the maidservant returned, and Mr. Chang, looking ashamed, apologized to her and did not mention again the object of his desire. But the maidservant said to him: 'What you told me, I dare not mention to my young mistress, nor will I let it be known to others. But as you know all the clan connexions of the Ts'ui family, why do you not seek marriage, basing your claim on your kindness to the family?'

Mr. Chang said: 'From the time when I was a child in arms my nature has been opposed to impropriety, and even when I have been living a life of luxurious ease I have never fixed my gaze on the fair sex. But though I have kept myself in restraint ever since then and ever after, to my unutterable surprise, yesterday at the feast, I felt it almost impossible to restrain myself. For the last few days, when I walk, I forget where to stop; when I eat, I forget to eat to the full. I fear that I cannot survive even for a day. If the marriage is to be arranged through a go-between, the sending of presents and the exchange of names will require three months at least, and at the end of that time you will find my corpse in a shop of rotten fish! What have you to say?'

The maidservant said: 'Miss Ts'ui has as her safeguard a character as virtuous as it is correct, and even those whom she respected dare not offend her with a flippant word; so any suggestion of a mere subordinate would not get a ready hearing from her. But she is good at literary composition and is always murmuring to herself lines of poetry which she is composing, and on which she dwells for long with a repining and longing look. Try her, sir, with a love lyric to arouse her feelings. If you do not act thus there is no other way.'

Mr. Chang was highly delighted and immediately composed a love poem of two stanzas, which he gave her. That evening Hung Niang came again with a piece of ornamented paper in her hand which she gave to Mr. Chang, saying: 'Miss Ts'ui has ordered me to hand you this.' The title of the poem (written on the paper) was 'Moonlight on the Evening of the Fifteenth' and the text was as follows:

> Await the moonlight at the Western Chamber,
> Where the door stands half open in the breeze.
> Whilst the shadows of the flower move on the wall,
> The Precious One may be coming!

Mr. Chang had a glimmering idea of what she meant. That evening was the fourteenth of the Second Moon. Near the eastern wall where the Ts'ui family lived there was an apricot tree, by which one could climb over the wall. On the evening of the fifteenth Mr. Chang, climbing up the tree, got over the wall. When he arrived at the Western Chamber the door was actually half open. Hung Niang was asleep on her bed, so Mr. Chang aroused her. Hung Niang was startled and said: 'Why have you come, sir?' Thereupon Mr. Chang deceived her by saying: 'The paper from Miss Ts'ui invited me to come. Report my arrival to her for me.'

After a short time Hung Niang returned and kept saying: 'She is coming. She is coming.' Mr. Chang was as pleased as he was astounded and thought he was sure to succeed. When Miss Ts'ui arrived, stately in her array and dignified in her look, she severely upbraided Mr. Chang, saying: 'Great, indeed, was your kindness in having saved from death our family! My dear mother entrusted her small son and young daughter to you. Why have you, making use of the services of an unscrupulous maidservant, sent me improper verses? At the beginning you displayed a righteous spirit in protecting others from outrage; but in the end you are acting outrageously in pursuing me. This is a case of changing one outrage for another. What is the difference between them? I should really like to hush up the matter, but to cover the wickedness of others is unrighteous. If I reveal the matter to my mother, I would then be showing ingratitude for your former kindness, which would be a sinister act. If I had sent my message by an underling, I am afraid it would not have revealed my true feelings. I therefore made use of this short poem as I wished to explain the matter in person. But still being afraid that you might hesitate, I wrote that vulgar and reckless poem with the object of making you certain to come. I cannot but feel ashamed of having had recourse to such an improper proceeding. My sole desire is now that you should restrain yourself within the bounds of propriety without exceeding them.' Having thus spoken, she at once vanished.

Mr. Chang remained dumbfounded for long. At last he climbed over the wall again and abandoned all hope. Several nights later, when Mr. Chang was sleeping alone near the veranda, he was suddenly awakened by some one, and, getting up startled and alarmed, he saw that Hung Niang had arrived with a folded bed-cover on her arm and a pillow in her hand. Touching Mr. Chang gently she said: 'She is coming. She is coming! Why are you asleep?' She then arranged the bed-cover and pillow and departed.

Mr. Chang, rubbing his eyes, sat up and assumed a serious attitude. For long he still thought it was a dream. But finally with a dignified air he waited. Soon Miss Ts'ui arrived, supported by Hung Niang. On her arrival, she looked as winsomely shy as she was beautifully attractive, and as delicate as if she could not move her limbs and support herself, presenting quite a different picture from her former dignified beauty. This was the evening of the eighteenth of the month. The slanting rays of the moon, glittering like crystal, gently illumined half the bed. Mr. Chang felt exalted and thought that a fairy had unexpectedly arisen from Heaven and not from among mortals. After a short time the temple bell sounded and dawn drew nigh. Hung Niang urged Miss Ts'ui to depart, and she, with gentle voice, cried plaintively until she left, supported as before by Hung Niang. During the whole night she had not uttered a syllable. Mr. Chang got up when dawn was breaking and said in doubt to himself: 'Was it a dream?' When daylight arrived, he observed that on his arm was the mark of her toilet, in his garments her fragrance still remained, and her tears, glittering like pearls, were still to be seen on the bedding.

More than ten days after this there was no further news of any kind. Mr. Chang was in the midst of composing a poem of thirty couplets entitled 'The Meeting of the Real Beauty' when Hung Niang happened to arrive, so he handed it to her to give to Miss Ts'ui. From this time henceforward she continued to receive him. In the morning he secretly came out and at night he secretly went in, and for about a month they were happy together in what was previously mentioned as the Western Chamber. Mr. Chang once asked what was the view of Madam Ts'ui regarding the matter, when Miss Ts'ui replied: 'Realizing that the affair is beyond remedy, she wishes to settle it by making the best of it.'

Before long Mr. Chang had to go to Ch'ang-an, and, prior to his departure, he explained the matter to her. Miss Ts'ui readily accepted the situation without raising any difficulties, but her sad, disappointed look would have moved any mortal. For two nights before his departure he had been unable to see her again, and went westwards. After some months he re-visited P'u and took up his abode with the Ts'ui family again for some months. Miss Ts'ui was skilful with her pen and excelled in literary composition, so that when Mr. Chang tried to get her writings to read without succeeding, he had recourse frequently to making use of his own compositions to induce her to give responses. But she paid little attention to them. Generally speaking, Miss Ts'ui's superiority was shown as follows. Though extremely talented (as she undoubtedly was) she assumed an air of ignorance; though as clever as she was eloquent, she seldom engaged in conversation; though she had very great affection for Mr. Chang, she never gave expression to it in words. She always appeared to be unacquainted with sorrow and discontent, and her countenance seldom revealed feelings either of joy or anger.

On one occasion, whilst playing her lute alone at night, the music she played was sad and full of sorrow. Mr. Chang furtively listened to it. When he asked her (to continue), she refused to play again. This made him more infatuated than ever. Soon again Mr. Chang, on account of the time fixed for the literary examination having arrived, had to go west-wards. On the evening of his departure he did not express in words again his feelings of love, but sadly sighed as he was at the side of Miss Ts'ui. She knew intuitively that they were about to separate, and with humble look and pleasant voice she gently said to him:

'To be first seduced and then abandoned is what is bound to happen! I dare not hate you on that account. But if you, who have seduced me, will without fail end the matter properly, that will be true kindness on your part. Then our solemn oath to be true to one another till death will be ful-filled. Why, then, must you be so sad at your departure now? You are so distressed and I have no means of relieving your feelings. But you once said that I played the lute well, and hitherto, through feeling ashamed, I have not been able to play to you. Now you are going away and have revealed the true feelings of your heart I will play the lute as you wished.'

So she played the tune of 'Rainbow Skirt and Feathered Garbs'. Before she had struck many notes the sorrowful tones were so mingled with sadness and so realistic that one would not have known it was merely music. All who heard it were moved to sighs. Miss Ts'ui abruptly stopped playing and, putting down the lute, covered her face with her hands and kept on weeping. She then returned to where her mother was and came no more. Next morning Mr. Chang set out on his journey.

The following year, not having been successful at the literary competitive examination, he stayed at the Capital. He therefore sent a letter to Miss Ts'ui to unfold his feelings, and her reply was roughly to the following effect:

'I have received your letter of kind inquiries in which your too great affection and love for me are revealed. My feelings of love are at present those of sorrow mingled with joy. In addition to your letter you have kindly presented me with a box of artificial flowers and a lip-rouge pad. As to the ornaments for adorning my head and the rouge for reddening my lips, although I am much indebted to you for your very great kindness, is there any one but you for whom

I would adorn myself? As I gaze at your presents, my longing for you is increased, only to end in greater sorrow and louder sighs than ever. Now that you have to undertake to carry on your literary studies at the Capital your duty is certainly to remain where you are so as to progress in your cultured pursuits. But, alas! I, the uncultured one, am left permanently alone and afar! Such is fate! Realizing this, what more can be said? Ever since last autumn I felt dazed as if something was absent. Amidst the bustle of social life I have tried to carry on conversations and to smile. When alone by myself at night my tears never cease to flow. And even in my sleep my dreams are almost always full of weeping at the sad thoughts of separation. Even if in them we are for a short time united again as formerly, the illusion of my soul is suddenly dispelled before our secret union had come go an end. Half my couch seems still warm, but when I think of our happy union it appears very far away.

'A year has quickly passed since I bade you farewell, though it seems but yesterday. Ch'ang An is a gay place where there are many attractions. How fortunate I am that you have not forgotten this lonely person, but ever have her in your thoughts. An unworthy and humble mortal as I am, I have nothing to offer you in return. As for the oath we took to be true to each other for ever, I will never for a moment forget.

'Formerly, on account of our relationship as cousins, we happened to meet at the feast. And having been led on by my maidservant, I gave you my affection, unable to restrain my feelings. You enticed me like the worthy of old who played the lute to win his love, but I offered no resistance by knocking out your teeth with a shuttle, as once happened. When I placed my pillow and mat at your service I was moved by feelings deep and profound. And in my foolish and young mind I thought I could trust myself to you for ever. But how could I have expected my union with you, not having been carried out with the usual proprieties, could not but result in the disgrace of surrendering myself and being unworthy "to hold for you the towel and comb", as a legal wife does. This will be to me a subject of everlasting regret until I die. Heavy with sighs, what can I say?

'If you, out of the kindness of your heart, will condescend to act as I, lonely and unworthy, desire, even after death I will be as grateful to you as when I was alive. Should you, as a man of wide vision, unmindful of private affections and abandoning what is petty for what is great, regard our pre-nuptial union as a disgraceful proceeding, and our oath as one that may be broken on account of its having been forced, then, though my bones may be dissolved and my body extinguished, my true and sincere love for you will never perish, and my spirit, wafted by the wind and wandering in the dew, will ever be faithful to you. Whether in life or death, such will be my unchanging love for you, and I can say no more. As I write this to you I sob and am unable to unfold all I feel. Take every care of your precious self! Of your precious self take every care!

'The jade ring that I played with in my childhood I send for you to wear. The jade is symbolical of firmness and purity without change. The ring is symbolical of eternity. I also send you a skein of coloured silk, a mill made of bamboo for grinding tea, which articles are as valueless as they are unworthy of your consideration. My wish is that you may be as pure as the jade and that your resolution may remain unbroken as the ring. The spots on the bamboo represent my tears, the entanglements of the silk my con-fused and sorrowful thoughts. I have used these articles to show my true feelings, in the hope that our love for each other may last for ever. My heart is ever with you though I am far away and there is no hope of our meeting. When both our thoughts are concentrated on feelings of sorrow and regret we still, though far separated, are united in spirit. Take every care of your precious self! The spring winds are very piercing, so it will be well for you to eat well. Be cautious in what you say and take care of yourself, and do not be concerned about me.'

Mr. Chang showed the letter to his intimates, so the matter became one of common knowledge among people of that time. One of his best friends, Mr. Yang Chü-yüan, was fond of writing poetry, so he composed a short poem of four lines entitled 'Miss Ts'ui'; and Mr. Yüan Chen of Honan also wrote in sixty lines a continuation of Mr. Chang's poem on 'Meeting the Real Beauty'. When the friends of Mr. Chang heard of the affair they were all, without exception, filled with surprise and astonishment. But Mr. Chang was determined to break off his association with the lady. Mr. Yüan Chen, being on especially intimate terms with Mr. Chang, asked him for an explanation. Mr. Chang replied:

'Generally speaking, all those whom Heaven has endowed with superlative beauty bring ill fate to themselves or to others. If the young lady of the Ts'ui family had happened to marry one of a rich and noble family, availing herself of her own bewitching charms and his devotion to her, she would either prove a benefactress or a monster, and I cannot tell which she may become. Formerly, the Emperor Hsin of the Yin Dynasty (1154–1135 B.C.) and the Emperor Yü of the Chou Dynasty (781–771 B.C.), though rulers of a great empire and in enjoyment of immense power, were ruined by a mere woman, who caused their whole population to turn against them and finally led to their death, and this up to the present time is still a subject of derision. My powers are not sufficient to overcome such bewitching evils; and it is for that reason that I have restrained my feelings.'

On this all those present sighed deeply.

More than a year afterwards Miss Ts'ui had married somebody else. Mr. Chang, who had also taken a wife, happened to pass by her abode, and sent a message to her through her husband saying that he wished to see her as her cousin. The husband conveyed the message, but she would not meet him as he desired. Mr. Chang was really very grieved and disappointed, as he showed in his face. She, having learned this, secretly indited a poem as follows:

Since I have been wasting away and the brilliance of my looks has been fading,
In endless anguish, I have tossed on my couch and have no heart to leave it.
It is not because I am ashamed to see any one that I do not come forth,
But because I am ashamed of you, who, having deserted me, have made me so melancholy and sorrowful.

She never granted him a meeting.

Several days later, when Mr. Chang was about to depart, she composed a second poem in order to bid him a last farewell:

> Deserted and abandoned, what can I say now—
> I, whom once you loved so fondly?
> But may your devotions of old
> Be bestowed on her whom now you love.

After this she was never heard of again. His contemporaries were loud in their praises of Mr. Chang for having so well repaired his former mistake. I have often, at meetings with my friends, referred to this matter. My intention has been to persuade those who become acquainted with it not to behave in the same way, and those who are so acting not to continue to be deluded. In the Ninth Moon of the Cheng Yuan Year, the official Li Kung-ch'ui spent the night at my country residence at Ching-an, and our conversation dealt with this matter.

Kung-ch'ui, astounded, expressed his surprise, and then composed the Song of Ying-ying in order to let the story be known. Ying-ying was the pet name of Miss Ts'ui when a child, so Kung-ch'ui made it the title of his song.